Anti-Aircraft Artillery

ANTI-AIRCRAFT ARTILLERY

Ian V. Hogg

The Crowood Press

First published in 2002 by
The Crowood Press Ltd
Ramsbury, Marlborough
Wiltshire SN8 2HR

British Library Cataloguing-in-Publication Data
A catalogue record for this book is available from the British Library.

ISBN 1 86126 502 6

Photograph previous page: American gunners at practice with a 37mm
gun in 1940, when it was still considered proper to wear rifles and
bayonets whilst wrestling with sight-setting and loading.

Typeset by Servis Filmsetting Ltd, Manchester

Printed and bound in Great Britain by Bookcraft, Bath

Contents

Introduction

Sixty years ago, if anyone spoke of 'anti-aircraft' you knew he meant guns. If he talked about 'air defence' then he was talking about aeroplanes. And if he mentioned 'missiles' he was a dangerous lunatic.

Today any one of those three terms appears to be interchangeable with the others and probably the last thing anybody thinks about is artillery, since, except for some odd corners of the earth where people are reluctant to throw anything away, medium and heavy air-defence artillery no longer exists, and in some countries there is precious little light artillery to be seen either. And yet in 1944, in Great Britain alone, the British army deployed 2,671 medium and heavy guns, and 2,608 light guns in the air defence role. These figures pale into insignificance when the comparable German strengths are examined; in September 1944, in Germany and the Western front, there were 10,225 medium and heavy guns and 18,508 light guns deployed; and the field armies in Italy and Russia deployed another 11,000 or so guns of both kinds.

If we go back a hundred years, then, of course, there were no aircraft and, not unnaturally, no anti-aircraft defences. But if you went back *ninety* years . . . you would be surprised to hear talk of anti-aircraft guns and, believe it or not, missiles.

This book is about Anti-Aircraft Artillery – 'Triple-A' as the US Army called it in the 1940s – but, as will become obvious, air defence has always been a complex business, shared originally between guns and aircraft, then with the later addition of searchlights, sound detectors, radar, and eventually missiles. All these things will have to be touched on as we trace the story.

But the guns were pre-eminent for the first three-quarters of the twentieth century and the light gun is still the most cost-effective air-defence weapon against the ground-attack aircraft or the helicopter. Admittedly, in the earliest days the guns fired an astronomical number of shells per aircraft brought down, but by the end of World War Two the ratio had come down to very creditable figures. It is an indisputable fact that during the flying bomb attacks on Antwerp in 1945, when only guns – no aircraft, no barrage balloons – were used, of the 4,883 flying bombs known to have been launched against Antwerp only 211 (4.35 per cent) got within 13km (8 miles) of the docks which were their aiming point. In the final days the guns were shooting down 97 per cent of the attackers.

On the face of it, and to the layman, anti-aircraft gunnery is impossible. The gunner is attempting to hit a target capable of moving in any of three directions (it used to be said that the only certain thing was that it wouldn't go backwards, but that was before the Harrier) at any speed from 160 to 1,300km/h (100–800mph) or more, at any height from above his head to 16km (10 miles) or more up in the sky. The odds against hitting a target under these conditions would appear to be astronomical. And yet, I have seen it done.

In the last months of 1940, when serious air raiding of London and its environs began, I was living in St Albans, which received sporadic attention from the Luftwaffe. One day a motor truck with a gun on it, manned by Naval ratings, suddenly appeared in the town. I know now that it was a 3-inch 20cwt AA gun dating from 1917. It had only the most rudimentary sights and no form of communication or target detection that anyone could see. Its job was simply to drive round during air raids, stop outside any air raid shelter it found and bang off a couple of rounds into the sky, just to put some heart into the occupants of the shelter and let them know that it wasn't entirely a one-sided affair. And since the greater part of the raids took place at night, the merry sailors were simply whacking rounds off into the darkness without knowing much about what was up there except that there weren't any of ours. And one night, half a minute or so after the firing of one of their morale-raisers, there was an explosion and a burst of flames in the sky, and a Heinkel 111 – or it might have been a Dornier 213 – plunged to the ground in flames.

I don't think those sailors ever bought a drink in St Albans after that. Hitting an aircraft under those conditions was probably the equivalent of a total stranger getting a hole in one at the St Andrews' seventeenth in thick fog.

As a result of this type of target the problems confronting the early anti-aircraft gunners were immense; in many armies it began as a branch of coast defence artillery, because the coast gunners were the only ones with experience of aiming at fast-moving targets and who had developed rudimentary scientific instruments to try and forecast where the target might be when the shell reached it. This sort of approach formed, if you like, one dimension of their solution, that of lateral movement, but the vertical aspect also had to be dealt with, as did the propensity of the target to turn, dive, climb and generally make a nuisance of itself. Had development continued under peacetime conditions, it is doubtful whether a workable solution would have been achieved in ten years, but as luck would have it the adolescence of air defence coincided with World War One. This meant that firstly there was an air of urgency that would otherwise have been absent, secondly that there was finance available which would certainly have been absent, and thirdly

that the wholesale recruitment and conscription of manpower brought numbers of scientists and engineers into the anti-aircraft field who would, in normal times, never have contemplated such employment. By 1918 all the combatant nations had air-defence artillery that could act as an effective deterrent and which could point with some pride at its wartime record.

By 1921 anti-aircraft artillery had almost vanished. Armies had been shorn from their wartime strengths to become skeletal forces; there would be no more wars, and in any case the money was needed for social reforms and political objectives. And since air defence was the last in, it was the first out as the armies shrank to their traditional and basic infantry–cavalry–artillery plus service corps form.

However, there were enough forward-looking individuals to see that what had been learned during the war was not forgotten, and that a cadre of artillerymen tended the shrine of air defence and studied, planned, and experimented against the day when the need would arise once more. Throughout the starvation years between 1920 and 1936, with assistance from commercial companies working virtually without profit, the technical problems were gradually brought under control, so that when the threat of war made itself obvious and the cash drawer was opened, the artillerymen of the various nations were ready with their designs and plans.

Even so, the air-defence artillery of 1939–45 would have shown little improvement over that of 1914–18 but for one thing – the invention of radar. Not only did this provide the air defences with accurate information on the height and position of their targets, but, and perhaps more importantly, it also opened the door to a new world of electronics, which was, eventually, to provide far more assistance than mere measurement of position. In 1939 it still took several hundred shells to obtain one hit; by 1945 this ratio had been improved to something in the order of 275 shells for one hit, and a great deal of that improvement was due to electronics.

After 1945 the reduction in air-defence artillery was less than it had been after 1918, but it was still quite substantial as money and man-power was poured into the development of guided missiles. Once these had reached a rea-sonable degree of efficiency, the heavy and medium anti-aircraft guns began to be phased out of most armies and by the mid-1960s they had completely vanished from virtually every major army outside the Soviet bloc. And once the scientists had perfected some smaller mis-siles, the light guns would go the same way.

But it didn't happen. Against a nuclear bomber flying at 50,000 feet a large and expen-sive guided missile, with a considerable logistic 'tail' is cost-effective. Against the nuisance ground attacker nipping in at zero feet to spray the place with cannon fire and a few rockets, missiles looked like being an enormous expense. And while this was still being agonized over, the

scientists came up with another breakthrough – electro-optical (or 'optronic') sighting systems, linked to compact computers, controlling small-calibre fast-firing automatic cannons. Suddenly there was an affordable air-defence system with a remarkably high hit-probability. And since that time, whilst the man-portable missile has gone into service in several guises, it has been supplemented in many armies by elec-tronically aided light artillery.

In the past ninety years a large number of anti-aircraft guns has been developed, many of which got little further than their prototype; regrettably, for reasons of space, it has not been possible to mention every one of them – the story of the multitude of German guns cobbled together during World War One alone would fill a book this size – but no weapon of significance has been ignored. By the same token, search-lights and aircraft have received the briefest of treatment in spite of their importance in the overall picture. Perhaps, one day . . .

1   Balloons and Aerostats

Aviation can be said to have begun when the Montgolfier brothers, Joseph and Jacques, made their pioneering ascent in a hot-air balloon in June 1783, and no sooner had they done so than the question arose of its utility in war. The answer was fairly obvious; from such a high viewpoint an observer could see far into the countryside, and in those days of marching armies he could pick out the tell-tale cloud of dust and glitter of accoutrements several miles distant and thus warn his own troops of the strength, direction, speed and possible time of arrival of the enemy. This surmise was rapidly confirmed when the first manned balloon flight was made in November 1783 by Pilâtre de Rozier and the Marquis d'Arlandes, who flew over Paris for about twenty minutes.

For the next ninety years or so the balloon was used sporadically by armies as an adjunct to observation and, not surprisingly, their opponents frequently took exception to this all-seeing eye and took pot shots at it with whatever weapon they had at hand. But none of it could be called 'anti-aircraft' since none of these weapons were intended for shooting at aerial objects and none of them were of much use at it.

In the Franco-Prussian War of 1870 the German troops had a small observation-balloon section, but there was difficulty in providing the necessary hydrogen gas and the two balloons accomplished little. It was not until Paris was besieged that the balloon achieved any useful purpose; with the city cut off, the Parisian postal authorities decided to use balloons filled with coal gas for carrying mail and, in all, some sixty-six balloons made their escape from the city, carrying between them sixty-six 'aeronauts' (pilots), 102 passengers and 9 tons of mail, as well as 409 carrier pigeons and six dogs.

On 7 October 1870 Leon Gambetta, Minister of the Interior and a noted political firebrand, escaped by balloon and joined the French Government at Tours, where he at once set about whipping up resistance to the Germans. This escape, and the possibility of other national figures sailing over the siege works to freedom, upset the Germans and on 14 November Alfried Krupp wrote to the Minister of War informing him that his company had built an anti-balloon gun to combat the Paris balloon problem and that six more guns would be ready within three weeks. These were all offered to the War Ministry free of charge and, by 25 November, the offer had been accepted and the first gun was on its way to Villacoublay near Paris, soon to be followed by the other six.

The Krupp *Balonabwehrkanone* (BaK) was the first gun specifically designed to combat an aerial target, and was a breech-loading 25mm rifle mounted on a pedestal on a light cart drawn by two horses. Contemporary pictures suggest that there were two varieties, one a simple flat cart, the other with a staging around the pedestal that allowed the gunner to climb up and down in order to keep the rifle's stock to his shoulder at any angle of elevation. In either type the weapon could be fired at elevations up to 85 degrees, while it was free to turn through 360 degrees so as to give the fullest possible field of fire.

On the face of it, the idea seems quite reasonable; the French balloons were 15m (50ft) in diameter, presenting quite a good target, but in practice the difficulties began to appear at once.

The first anti-aircraft gun appears to have been this heavy rifle mounted upon a cart, devised by Krupp to attack French balloons in 1870.

In the first place, the rifle had no more than the simple V-backsight and barleycorn-foresight as used on the contemporary needle-gun rifle of the infantry, so that there was no accurate way of adjusting the aim to allow for the movement or varying range of the balloon. Secondly, the projectile was a solid lead bullet that left no sign of its passage through the air, and where it went in relation to the balloon was not known to the gunner. Thirdly, there was the problem of placing the gun in the right place to shoot at a balloon, a problem which was attacked by dispersing the guns around the city harnessed up and having them gallop like a fire brigade when a balloon was seen to be rising. In spite of all these difficulties there was a small degree of success; some of the aeronauts were dismayed to have half-pounds of lead whistling past them, while others were unfortunate enough to have the balloons punctured by shots, one being so badly perforated that it was forced to descend in the Prussian lines. But, on the whole, the success rate was low and the French soon neutralized the guns by launching their balloons at night. Dwindling supplies of gas and materials for construction of the balloons also had its effect upon the frequency of flights and,

Another contemporary picture of the Krupp anti-balloon rifle shows this entirely different carriage with a staging to permit the gunner to stay on his feet at all angles of fire. This may well have been developed as a modification in the light of field experience.

of course, the surrender of Paris on 27 January 1871 effectively ended the anti-balloon problem. The guns were withdrawn and were apparently given to the German Navy, who used them for some years as boat landing guns before scrapping them. One remains, tucked away in an obscure corner of a small museum in Berlin.

From this time onwards balloons became more or less standard items in most armies, though in many cases they were more in the nature of experimental devices than practical service equipment. Such matters as the best shape and size, the method of hanging the observer's basket, the method of generating gas in the field, problems of mooring and sheltering balloons – these were the fundamental problems of the period and they occupied the time of the embryo aviators to the exclusion of anything very valuable in the tactical sense. The first British use was of spherical observation balloons in South Africa in 1900. In typically British style, they were made of gold-beater's skin (the peritoneum of the ox) and were *very* expensive as well as being difficult to repair and maintain in the South African climate. Nevertheless they proved useful on a number of occasions, and the military balloon became a familiar sight on exercises in the first decade of the twentieth century.

Towards the turn of the century the dirigible balloon began to supplant the earlier free balloons; it should be pointed out that 'dirigible' indicates the ability to steer and direct the balloon, and implies its provision with an engine and rudder, and not, as is often supposed, the existence of a rigid framework to carry the gas bags. Dirigibles could be propelled

in specific directions and were no longer at the mercy of the wind; this facility immediately led military men to think about propelling them in the direction of the enemy for the purpose of gathering information. Some thinkers went even further and proposed using them to drop bombs, though this was felt to be scarcely practical in the early days – the dirigibles had enough to worry about in lifting themselves off the ground, without adding to their troubles with loads of bombs.

Scarcely had the dirigible established itself than the Wright brothers made their historic flight at Kitty Hawk, and the age of the heavier-than-air craft had dawned. This, in its early days, was considered to be even less likely to have a future than the dirigibie and it was almost entirely ignored by military experimenters, who felt that the greater potential

37 Battery, Royal Field Artillery advancing towards Johannesburg in 1900, accompanied by the Balloon Corps.

lifting power of the dirigible would prove to have more practical value in the military role. Within a very few years though, the boot was on the other foot and the aeroplane was being heralded as the most likely form of military craft, due to its greater agility and, what promised to be important, the smaller size it presented as a target.

With all this activity in the air, questions began to be asked about the possibilities of military use of aircraft and, as a corollary, what the land and sea services could do to counter them. It was generally agreed that aviation's principal – if not only – function in war would be the acquisition of information; just as the balloon had extended the field of view, so the dirigible and the aeroplane would extend the view of the modern commander even deeper into enemy territory, and, pertinent to England, the sea was no barrier. German or French aircraft could fly across the Channel and peer down into dockyards and naval bases, selecting targets for naval bombardment or checking on the presence or absence of warships. Obviously, this was something that had to be prevented, and in the mid-1900s the armies of the major nations began to take an interest, if only an academic one, in the matter of air defence. The general view seemed to be that, whilst the aircraft seemed unlikely to be of much value, some gestures had to be made to satisfy the public. Indeed, as late as 1913, a senior officer gave as his considered opinion:

> I think we are making altogether too much of a bogey, a bogey made in Germany, over this air business. One thing I am fairly certain of and that is that at the end of the first week [of war] there will not be many airships or aeroplanes left, and if there are, the pilots, unless the nature of pilots is changed, will be incapable of further action – their nerves will have gone.

As is very commonly the case, private enterprise made the first overt moves. In 1909, at the Frankfurt International Exhibition, two German gun makers of high repute exhibited a number of 'balloon guns', and the evidence that such respected names as Krupp and Erhardt were sufficiently impressed by the aerial threat to design and build guns was enough to stimulate military interest to the point of actually doing something.

At Frankfurt the centre of the Great Hall was given over to a large display mounted by Fried, Krupp of Essen and Rheinische Metallwaaren-und Maschinenfabrik AG of Düsseldorf, makers of the Erhardt designs of ordnance. Krupp showed three weapons: a 65mm gun on a field carriage, a 75mm gun on a motorized carriage, and a 105mm gun suitable for shipboard mounting. Erhardt displayed a 50mm gun on two different motorized mountings, one fully armoured and the other partially armoured. These designs were of considerable interest insofar as they revealed their designers' views on anti-aircraft tactics as much as their views on ordnance construction.

Krupp's 65mm gun resembled a conventional field piece of the day, on a two-wheeled carriage with a solid trail and no shield, but it was capable of elevating to 70 degrees and could pitch its 4kg (9lb) shell to 5,500m (18,000ft) altitude. The most unusual feature was the mounting of the wheels on hinged axle extensions so that, when the gun was positioned ready to fire, the wheels could be swung round to the front of the mounting to lie parallel with the axle. The trail end was then pinned to the ground by a stake, so that by manhandling the wheels the whole weapon could be pivoted in a circle around the trail end, giving an all-round field of fire, considered to be vital in shooting at a rapidly-moving target.

Krupp's second weapon, the 75mm 'motor gun', demonstrated another approach to the moving target problem, the solution in this case being the ability to move the mounting and position it rapidly so as to intercept the flight path of the aircraft or, in another view, to take

The Krupp 9-pounder (65mm) gun of 1909, showing how the wheels could be swung forward so as to allow the entire weapon to be rapidly traversed in a complete circle.

to the road and chase the target. The gun was installed on the bed of a 50hp motor truck, capable of a speed of 45km/h (28mph). With 75 degrees of elevation the 5.5kg (12lb) shell had a maximum ceiling of 6,500m (21,000ft) and the gun could be traversed through 360 degrees on the truck so as to cover the entire horizon.

Krupp's greatest technical problem was that of absorbing the recoil blow of the gun when it fired, so that the truck was not hammered to pieces; a rough calculation shows that the recoil force would be in the order of 13 tons (13,000kg). This was dealt with by adopting a system recently proposed, that of differential or dynamic recoil. The gun, prior to opening fire, was winched back in its recoil cradle against the pressure of a compressed-air piston and then held in this fully recoiled position, where it was loaded. On pressing the firing lever the gun was released and allowed to run forward under the propulsive force of the compressed air. As it approached the fully-forward position the car-tridge was fired. Thus the explosion and its reaction on the gun had first of all to arrest the forward movement of the 550kg (1200lb)

weight of the gun, then reverse the motion and begin the conventional recoil stroke, at the end of which the gun was again held ready for loading. The result of this system was to reduce the recoil blow to about a quarter of the normal figure.

The Rheinische Metallwaaren- und Maschinenfabrik AG (who later adopted the shorter form 'Rheinmetall GmbH' by which they are still known) exhibited another approach to the mobility and recoil problems. Their 50mm gun, which was conventional enough, was mounted in a turret in an armoured car. To quote from a contemporary report:

To protect the car, its equipment and gun detachment from hostile fire it is armoured throughout, including the wheels, with 3mm [0.1in] of nickel steel. The entrance, the peep-hole for the driver, and the embrasures in the sides can all be closed and the forward part of the car shut down. The gun with its armoured turret can be revolved on a turntable and the embrasures are provided with shutters.

The 'Platformwagen' was the most popular solution to the anti-balloon problem, since it could be rapidly moved and, in the last resort, could chase the target. This was the Krupp 75mm Model of 1908.

Another Krupp design of 1908 was this 71mm gun inside an armoured turret. It looks as if it would have been somewhat cramped inside the turret, especially when the gun recoiled.

The Ehrhardt armoured 5cm balloon gun had the gun in a small turret, but left a reasonable amount of room for the crew to operate under armour.

While all this seemed quite reasonable, there were a few doubters who objected that they failed to see much point in armouring a balloon gun: the chances of a balloon or aircraft mounting any armament to duel with the ground gun were remote and there seemed little likelihood of the weapon operating so far forward as to come under fire from enemy ground troops. An alternative reason for the armour was advanced by Colonel Bethell, a well-known contemporary writer on ordnance design, namely that the addition of armour made the vehicle heavier and more robust, allowing it to absorb the recoil of the 50mm gun without having to resort to the complications of the differential recoil system.

Whether or not Bethell's theory is correct – and it has some validity – the fact remains that Rheinmetall also demonstrated a second model of 'half-armoured car', which used the same basic chassis but carried an open body of armour plate with the gun on a pedestal at the rear. This must have reduced the weight by a considerable amount, but there was still no move to adopt the differential recoil.

If the design of guns allowed scope for differing points of view, this was nothing when compared with the divergence of opinion over the projectiles to be fired from anti-balloon guns. The dirigible was a peculiar target; although it was of a fair size and presented a fine aiming mark, its thin fabric was so unresisting that there promised to be great difficulty in designing an impact fuze sufficiently sensitive to detonate the shell upon striking the balloon but safe enough to survive being fired from the gun. The amount of damage done to a balloon had to be considerable in order to have any useful effect. In May 1909 the German Army had staged a fairly conclusive trial at the Jüterbog Infantry School, near Berlin. Two detachments of infantry were deployed, one armed with service Mauser rifles and the other with Maxim machine guns, their target being a captive balloon 15m (50ft) long at a range of 1,250m (4,000ft). The riflemen opened fire first and discharged 4,800 rounds in five minutes, producing no visible result. The Maxim gunners then took their turn, firing 2,700 rounds in two and a half minutes, still without any apparent result. The balloon was then hauled down and was found to have been pierced in seventy-six places, the fabric having tended to close itself after the passage of the bullet by a combination of its elasticity and the internal gas pressure.

The conclusions drawn from this test reinforced the previously held opinion that a balloon could not be brought down by infantry fire alone and that the only time infantry should be allowed to attempt to engage an aerial target was when they were close enough to be able to hit the pilot or observers. The task of actually destroying the balloon was one that should be left to the artillery. And having said that, the

The Ehrhardt 'half armoured' balloon gun, a 14-pounder (75mm), went to the other extreme and gave practically no protection at all to the crew.

Another Ehrhardt 75mm gun solution of 1909 placed the gun in a revolving armoured box at the rear of the vehicle chassis. This one appeared at the Frankfurt Exhibition of 1909.

The Ehrhardt 5cm gun removed from its turret and placed on a pedestal mount.

German Army more or less sat back and waited for the gun makers to come up with some suitable answer.

The 'standard' artillery shell of the period was the shrapnel shell, a hollow casing filled with lead bullets and a small charge of gunpowder; actuated by a time fuze, the charge ejected the bullets forward in a cone, moving slightly faster than the remaining velocity of the shell. It was the ideal projectile for an attack on troops in the open; for 'protected' targets, such as buildings or defensive works, the high-explosive shell was produced, though in 1909 this was at a relatively primitive stage of development. The high-explosive shell was provided with an impact fuze so that it detonated upon striking the target, or the ground at the end of its flight. Some armies, who reserved high-explosive shells for their siege howitzers, preferred a shell with a hard point and with the fuze inserted in the base of the shell, so that it would smash through masonry or concrete before detonating inside the protected area.

A third type of shell was striving for acceptance at that time – the 'universal shell', first developed in Germany. This was an attempt to have the best of both worlds, by combining a shrapnel shell with a high-explosive charge, and there were two systems on offer. In the first system the shrapnel bullets (lead balls) were

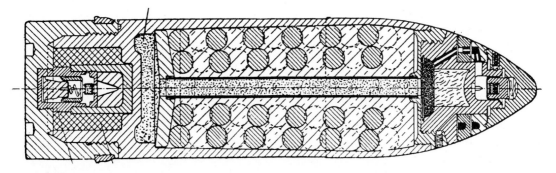

A drawing of the Krupp 'universal' shell of 1910. The lead-shrapnel balls are packed in TNT. The time fuze will flash down the central tube and fire the small gunpowder charge, expelling the bullets through the shell nose and igniting the TNT to give a black smoke cloud. If the shell hits anything solid, the base fuze will detonate the TNT and burst the shell, spreading bullets, blast and shell fragments in all directions.

held inside the shell in a matrix of TNT instead of the usual resin and the fuze was designed so that it operated as a time fuze if the user wanted a shrapnel effect or as a detonating impact fuze if he wanted a high-explosive effect. The operation of the time fuze fired the gunpowder charge in the bottom end of the shell and ejected the shrapnel bullets in the usual manner, igniting the TNT so that it burned and gave off a cloud of black smoke to indicate the point of burst. Setting the fuze for impact, however, cause the TNT to be detonated, blasting the shell fragments and lead bullets in all directions around the point of impact.

The other option had the bullets reduced in number so as to leave space for a cylindrical container filled with TNT to go down the centre of the shell and carry the fuze. In this design the result was the same whether the fuze was set for time or impact operation: the expelling charge was ignited and blew the shrapnel balls out of the nose of the shell, and at the same time blew the explosive charge holder out as well. The fuze, having functioned on time, was still carrying an unfired impact element and this would detonate the TNT charge as soon as it hit anything.

Generally speaking, the high-explosive shell was not considered a suitable projectile for anti-aircraft fire, since to be effective it had to hit the target. And the target, in this case, was, to say the least of it, flimsy and not likely to present sufficient resistance to the shell to make the fuze function. Shrapnel, on the other hand, was not required to hit the target. You merely had to burst the shell somewhat short of the target and the expanding cone of bullets would do the rest. Universal shells appeared to hold the best promise, since they gave the shrapnel effect but had the bonus that the explosive charge could possible prove decisive should the shell actually strike the target and meet sufficient resistance.

The principal drawback to all this theory was the hard fact that only the shrapnel shell was practicable. Development of fuzes and shell designs that would unfailingly detonate TNT

was in its infancy, and outweighing all other considerations was the question of what was likely to happen if the fuze, for any reason, decided to function before the shell had left the gun barrel. With a shrapnel shell a premature functioning was no great matter; there was a muffled bang and a shower of lead balls came out of the gun muzzle, followed by the empty shell body. With a shell filled with TNT the consequences would be vastly different; a loud bang and the disintegration of the gun barrel into several pieces, and probably the death of two or three men of the gun detachment. So fuzes had to be designed which were 'bore safe' and completely incapable of functioning until they had left the gun. After which they had to be sensitive enough to function on striking a piece of thin fabric or a slender wooden spar in the structure of an airship or aeroplane. The two demands were compatible, but only after several years of experiment and failure. In the meantime, shrapnel and the time fuze appeared to be the only answer.

But before the anti-aircraft debate got as far as discussing ammunition, there were some more basic questions to be answered. Such as the point raised by Brigadier General Stone, Commander, Royal Artillery, South Western District, in his report on the use of aircraft in the 1912 manoeuvres:

The impossibility of distinguishing friendly from hostile aeroplanes was evident to everyone, and, so far as my own observation went, no attempt was made to fire on them for this reason. I have not come across any really practicable suggestion for getting over this difficulty either at manoeuvres or in war. The tendency is to regard artillery, machine gun and infantry fire merely as a means of keeping aircraft at a respectful height and thus increase their difficulties of observation, and to look to the armed aeroplane itself to put other aircraft out of action in the air. The identification question, however, still remains a difficulty.

And, of course, there was the ever-present question of finance and how much could we afford? A very percipient retired gunner, Major Hawkins, wrote in the 'Proceedings of the RA Institute' early in 1913:

> At present we must rely on guns for defence, and the only question is what expenditure is justifiable. It must be remembered that although we must, in the near future, build an aerial fleet or we cease to be an Empire, and granted that the proper opponent of the airship is the airship, still we need a special armament for immediate needs as a defence against existing threats . . .

The good Major then went on to propose a system of protecting dockyards with guns on fixed emplacements, pointing towards the sea so that the debris from the shells would fall safely into the water, and pointed out that:

> One realizes, of course, the necessary risks to the population of using guns at all, but a plain man can see no other possibility at present; had we kept our proper place in the van of scientific progress by judicious expenditure in the last few years, we might well have had mobile aerial torpedoes, worked by wireless currents, which would make the approaches to our dockyards as dangerous to dirigibles at night as the three-mile limit is to hostile ships of the line. The civil population, of course, must be warned in time of war that they leave their own houses after dark at their own risk . . .

In discussing the technicalities of the anti-aircraft gun, he made one or two comments that, had they been more closely observed at the time, would have saved a great deal of effort in later years:

> Sighting: The crux is the invention of an auto-sight, which does not seem to be a difficult matter. If the apparatus were found to be too cumbersome to be installed on the gun mounting, it might be used separately, the gun being trained and elevated by electricity. The extra expense would be repaid by increased accuracy over any other system.
>
> Lookouts: A good look-out, both national and local, is essential. The Navy would no doubt have special patrols about our coasts that are liable to the approach of dirigibles. Once reported, a good estimate of their destination could be made by taking into account the time and direction of the wind. Local look-out stations would require rough instruments of the astrolabe type as well as oriented charts. By combining two or three messages, the officer at the guns would know exactly where to expect his target.

Major Hawkins returned to the subject later in the year pointing out that:

> . . . one often sees it asserted by lawyers and others that unfortified towns will not be bombarded in wartime by a civilized Power, but surely it is allowable to destroy railway stations that are being used, or might be used, for the conveyance of troops. One rather shudders at what one imagines would be the state of London, or any other city, after airships had been trying to destroy all the railway stations in a bad light by dropping quantities of high explosives on them.

After which he went on to point out the possibility of developing an armour-piercing bomb capable of defeating the deck armour of warships, and prophesying that the aircraft would eventually render the battleship and the big gun obsolete. He ended his article by asking:

> . . . is there any reason why an improved seaplane should not carry torpedoes? If not, it would seem that she might well be a cheap and effective substitute for the torpedo boat. One would think that it would not be difficult for

her to discharge her torpedo without actually alighting on the water.

Which probably got him black-balled by the Navy, since he never appeared in the pages of the *Proceedings* again.

In November 1913, after a lecture on 'Aircraft in War' at the Royal Artillery Institution, there was a public discussion at which some of the problems which trial shots at balloons and kites had revealed:

[Lt Col C Battiscomb]: I doubt if at 3,500 feet we could do much good by shooting at an aeroplane. I think possibly we might do something with an airship, but it is a very difficult target to range on. You cannot tell at all where your shell is going. If you see your shell bursting beyond the airship, you cannot tell whether your shell is bursting on the upward flight or whether it has passed the top of its trajectory and burst on the downward flight; whether it has passed up one side of the airship and come down behind it, or gone up on the top side of the airship unless you have some sort of smoke trace.

By this time, too, there had been some practical experience of the use of aircraft in warfare but not, unfortunately, sufficient to allow sound conclusions to be drawn. In 1911 Italy had gone to war with Turkey, and the Italians used aircraft for reconnaissance for the first time. One aviator flew over Tripoli at 2,500 feet and suffered seven shots through his aeroplane, though luckily none hit a vital component or injured him. In 1912 the French deployed a number of aircraft against Moroccan tribesmen and two of their aviators who flew too close to hilltops occupied by Moroccans were wounded by rifle fire.

And then, in 1912, came the First Balkan War, when Bulgaria, Greece, Montenegro and Serbia decided to evict Turkey-in-Europe from Europe. The Bulgarians rounded up a number of pri-

vately owned aircraft and their owners were commissioned into the Bulgarian or Greek armies. A Bulgarian named Constantin, flying across the Chatalja Lines outside Constantinople, was struck by a rifle bullet and killed. His aircraft crashed and his body was found alongside it, with more bullet-holes in the fabric. His altimeter read a maximum height of 3,500 feet, though there was no evidence of what height he was flying when he met his death. He therefore has the melancholy distinction of being the first aviator to die from anti-aircraft gunfire.

Brigadier General Stone now seems to have become a leading expert upon aviation matters and was invited to address the Scottish Aeronautical Society in November 1913. Whereupon he drew some discouraging conclusions:

Aeroplanes have already been deployed in war for the purpose of discharging bombs, but the experience of the Italians in Tripoli and subsequent experience in the Balkan War does not lead us to anticipate that the use of explosive or incendiary bombs by aeroplanes is likely to develop on an extensive scale, but rather that it will be restricted to attempts to stampede horses and create a certain amount of confusion by moral effect, rather than by destruction of personnel or material on any appreciable scale . . . it seems clear that provided there is artillery on the spot, ready to open fire, hostile aeroplanes can be kept at a height of 4,000 feet, from which elevation it is most unlikely that any missiles could be discharged with accuracy.

He then continued at some length to discuss the Rules of War and confidently predicted that there was no danger to the civil population since no civilized country would dream of dropping bombs upon anything other than a purely military target.

These various opinions and conclusions were not confined to Britain; foreign military journals, extracts from which appeared in several British equivalents, all showed that every country that had given any thought to air defence had been confronted with the same problems. One result of this was a growing feeling that one of the greatest hurdles to be overcome was that of the expense of developing an entirely new kind of artillery, with entirely new ammunition and fire control problems, which could, at the moment, scarcely be imagined. This led to the belief that perhaps the easiest and cheapest solution would be to develop a gun that could be employed as a normal field artillery piece until such time as an enemy air threat developed, when it could, by a few turns of the appropriate handles, be elevated and controlled so as to act as an air-defence weapon. The idea grew fairly rapidly, and it was to take a very long time to die, since designers were reluctant to accept what practical gunners told them: that such dual-purpose guns usually inherited all the defects of both parents and none of the advantages of either.

In the early days a number of experiments were carried out against balloons and kites towed by galloping horses, and some encouraging results were achieved, but closer examination of the manner in which these trials were conducted usually reveals that the targets were at no very great height and some considerable distance away from the guns, so that they became fairly easy shrapnel targets. The prime defect was that the field gun of the day was invariably light in weight, so as to be capable of being towed all day by six horses, and this meant a somewhat spartan approach to carriage design, with limited traverse (usually no more than 5 or 6 degrees right and left of centre) and limited elevation (15 degrees was normal) due to a simple pole trail which prevented the breech going any lower.

As a result, once the target moved past the range of the traversing gears, the whole carriage had to be rapidly shifted, and once the height of the target exceeded the maximum possible elevation of the gun, the battle was over.

Various design expedients were tried. The Krupp design using wheels that swivelled to become traversing devices has already been mentioned and was copied by several other designers. To allow more elevation the trail was made in an open form so that there was room for the breech to pass through and thus allow the muzzle to rise, but this brought more problems in its train. The recoil systems used with field guns were designed to operate at low angles of elevation, and suddenly cocking the gun up to 70 degrees or more meant that the recuperator mechanism, whether it was spring or pneumatic, was not capable of pulling the gun back into the firing position after recoil. Moreover, simply allowing the gun breech to descend between the sides of the trail did not make it easy to load, and it became necessary to depress the muzzle and raise the breech in order to allow reloading.

A French designer solved that problem; Colonel Deport had been one of the designers of the famous French 75mm, 1897 field gun, and after his retirement in the early 1900s he had gone to work for the Forges de Chatillon designing artillery for export. In 1911 he produced his masterpiece, the split trail. Instead of a one-piece strut behind the gun, the trail was now in two pieces, hinged to the axle-tree so that they could be splayed out, leaving sufficient room inside the legs for men to stand and operate the breech and load the gun at any angle of elevation. It also permitted a wide amount of traverse, since the recoil force passed down the splayed trail-leg and did not attempt to overturn the entire gun. The Americans, then in the opening stages of development of a new field gun, took to this idea with alacrity, and proceeded to develop their 3-inch M1916 gun (as it was forecast to be) as a dual-purpose field/AA gun, with a maximum elevation of 53 degrees and with 45 degrees of traverse.

But, of course, all these clever modifications had the same defect: they added weight behind the horse team. So the more the designers and

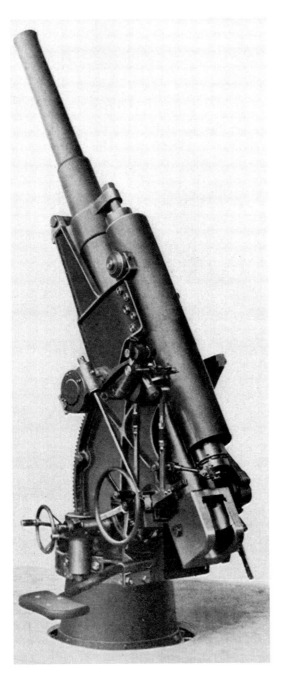

A Krupp 12-pounder (75mm) gun for static mounting in dockyards and fortresses.

artillerymen looked at the problem, the more it became apparent that the only reasonable solution was to develop specialized artillery for the anti-aircraft task; the dual-purpose gun was not a practical proposition.

The engineers went off to start designing guns; the artillerymen now had to turn their minds to the question of fire control: how to acquire the target, and how to aim at it. There were two ways of detecting the air target – you either saw it coming or you heard it coming. To rely on visual acquisition meant having an 'air sentry' peering at the sky all day long, and experience soon showed that such a sentry needed changing much more often than the traditional kind, since there is a hypnotic effect in staring into the sky for long period, such that when a target appears you fail to see it.

The only drawback to using sound to detect an approaching aircraft was that the aircraft of the first few years did not make very much noise; their engines were small and by the standards of today very quiet. The only advantage was that, outside the immediate battle zone, the world was a much quieter place in those days and even a quiet motor could be detected by the unaided ear. In a similar manner the average aeroplane was a small machine and difficult for the air sentry to see; a fact balanced by the rarity of aeroplanes so that any moving article in the sky would be fairly quickly spotted.

Sound appeared to be the better bet and it was also operable in darkness, so sound detection was a subject for some study and experimentation. But attempting to detect a moving object by sound brings its own problems. The speed at which sound travels is about 335m (1,100ft) per second – the exact figure varies according to the height above sea level of the observer, the air density and humidity and sundry other factors. This is about 1,200km/h or 750mph. If we assume an aircraft becomes audible at 15km (9 miles) distance, then the sound of the machine will reach us some 45 seconds later. If the machine is flying at

200km/h (125mph), then it will have come 2.5km (2 miles) closer to us in the time it took for the noise to reach us. If we now make some allowance for getting the men on to the guns, making the necessary calculations, setting fuzes, loading and laying the guns, and then firing, it becomes obvious that we are not going to get much shooting done before the aircraft is overhead or even past us and rapidly disappearing. In fact we have just four and a half minutes from the first sound of the machine to it passing overhead.

Once this point is appreciated it becomes a fairly easy arithmetical task to take it into account when working out where the aircraft might be; it also concentrates the mind on to the question of somehow improving your sound detection system beyond the range of the unaided human ear.

Having been warned by sound, the target still had to be acquired by eye so that the gun layers had something at which to aim. Given that, correction for lateral motion was simply a matter of 'aiming off'; setting the sight so that when the sight was on the target, the gun was pointed some distance in front of it proportional to its speed. This was a well-understood process, even though the amount of aim-off required for an aeroplane was larger than gunners were accustomed to setting. What caused the greatest amount of head scratching was the question of elevation. Without delving too deeply, the problem lay with the 'non-rigidity of the trajectory'. The trajectory described by a shell when firing at a target on the ground was well understood and easily visualized. But this only held good at the low elevations used by field guns of the day. Once you elevated the gun to 70 or 80 degrees, the trajectory did not remain the same shape and became almost impossible to visualize; and since the flight of the shell was invisible, when it finally burst, as we have already seen some of the early critics observe, you had no idea what course it had taken to get to that point. And it was hard for dyed-in-the-wool field and coast gunners to conceive a method of gunnery that did not depend upon visual estimates of the relative positions of shell burst and target and deductions therefrom. Most people would have thrown up their hands in despair, but gunners are a persevering breed and they were determined to make the system work. And while they pondered and drew diagrams and argued, the gun makers began putting their ideas to work.

The first purpose-built anti-aircraft gun, as opposed to a converted or modified field gun, was developed in Britain's Woolwich Arsenal in 1913–14 at the behest of the Royal Navy. Early in 1913 they had become apprehensive of the possibility of a surprise air attack on various Naval installations and had asked the army to provide a suitable gun to protect their extensive magazines at Chattenden, north of Rochester. The only weapon which the army could offer was their 6-inch 30cwt siege howitzer on its siege platform; and the reason they offered this most inappropriate weapon was simply because it was the only thing in the armoury which would elevate to 70 degrees. Four of these guns were duly installed, but the Admiralty were so shaken by this that they immediately set about organizing the design of their own gun for the purpose of defending dockyards, magazines and other sensitive spots in the naval empire. The design was such that the gun could be mounted on ships or be bolted down to a holdfast ring anchored in concrete, and it laid down the basic shape of most of the anti-aircraft guns that followed it.

The 3-inch gun was quite unremarkable for its day, a built-up gun with a vertical sliding semi-automatic breechblock. The block itself was a little out of the ordinary; instead of simply being a flat-sided steel block, it had the sides cut with saw-toothed vertical grooves, matching similar grooves in the breech ring, so as to give multiple thrust surfaces and so spread the chamber pressure force. The block was controlled by a crank on a shaft, and the block

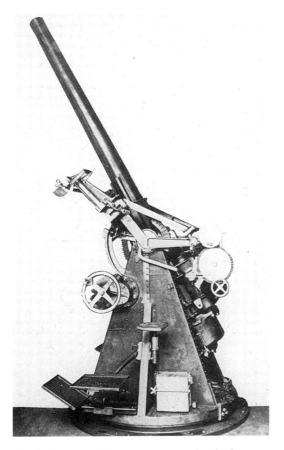

The British 3-inch 20cwt gun more or less laid down the general shape and appearance of AA guns for several years. This was the static version for ships or ground emplacement.

remained closed as the gun recoiled. As the gun ran out again the shaft was rotated by a cam on the fixed cradle of the carriage, so opening the block and ejecting the spent cartridge case. The block opened against the pressure of a spring and, once open, the extractors held it so until the next round was loaded. As the rim of the cartridge struck the extractors, so the block was released and the spring closed it. The firing mechanism, inside the block, had been cocked on the opening movement and the gun was thus ready to fire as soon as the block had closed.

The mounting was a fairly simple hollow pedestal with a pair of upright sides at the top, ending in trunnion bearings into which the gun and its cradle fitted. The barrel could be elevated to 90 degrees and the traverse was an unlimited 360 degrees. The sights were based on elevation angles rather than on range, a telescope was fitted and there was reasonable provision for lateral aim-off. On the whole it was a well thought-out, well-built design and it was approved for service in March 1914; by this time the army was working on its own design, but the 3-inch 20cwt Mark 1 was actually introduced as 'common' equipment, for use by both the army and the navy. Although approved, finance for its manufacture was slow in appearing, and by August 1914 only four had been built; two went to Chattenden to replace the 6-inch howitzers, one went to the Royal Gunpowder Factory at Waltham Abbey, and the fourth was installed to guard the cordite magazines at Purfleet on the River Thames.

The army's development had taken two paths. In about 1911 the Ordnance Board had reached the conclusion that there were two possible lines of approach: a fast-firing small-calibre gun to put a large number of impact-fuzed shells into the air very quickly, in the hope that at least one of them would strike the target; and a larger and more powerful gun to fire shrapnel or high-explosive shells that, with a time fuze to burst them at the right height, would have a larger area of effect in the sky so that even a 'near miss' might do some damage. Designs were called for and experiments ordered. At that time the Royal Artillery was sub-divided into three branches, Horse, Field and Garrison, and the question now arose of who should man such new equipment if it appeared. On the grounds that they were more used to shooting at moving targets, since they manned the coastal defence guns, it seemed that the Garrison Artillery should furnish the anti-balloon force, but another viewpoint was that, since these weapons would have to accompany the field armies and since everybody knew the

Garrison gunners were rooted in concrete and never went outside their forts, it was obviously the task of the Field branch.

What clinched the argument was the belief that the prime target of enemy aircraft would be dockyards and naval bases; and since it was the role of the Garrison Artillery to provide defence for these places, provision of air defence seemed to be automatically their responsibility. Whatever the arguments, it was the Garrison Artillery who moved first. In 1913, at their Western District School of Gunnery at Golden Hill Fort on the Isle of Wight, they took a one-pounder Maxim 'Pom-pom' automatic gun and mounted it on to a pedestal mount from a six-pounder anti-torpedo-boat gun, increasing the amount of elevation possible. This gun was then installed at Needles Battery, on the western tip of the island, and a destroyer of the Royal Navy steamed back and forth at high speed off the shore, towing a kite. With a maximum speed across the front of about 30 knots (55km/h) and a range of about 6,500ft (2,000m) the angular movement was well within the capabilities of the gun mounting and the gun layer, and the practice scored a reasonable number of hits.

While this test showed that the pom-pom was a suitable weapon, it also underlined a problem to which one or two far-sighted men had already called attention – the question of what happened to the shells that missed the target and continued on their way, to fall to earth fuzed and primed to detonate as soon as they struck something. In 1910 Colonel Bethell, in his book *Modern Guns and Gunnery*, had dismissed the problem as being of little account:

> It has been objected to balloon guns in general that our own troops would be endangered by the shells falling on their heads. This objection is, however, unsound; even if the balloon is attacked by a rival dirigible or aeroplane, it has to be destroyed by projectiles of some sort. And it matters little to the soldier below

whether a shell that falls on his head from a height of 5,000 feet weighs one pound or twelve. Moreover the Krupp 12-pounder, for instance, ranges some 8 miles at 45 degrees elevation, so that at any rate the troops in the vicinity of the gun would not suffer. Finally, since the object in view is to bring down some tons of balloon or some hundredweights of aeroplane from the sky, the incidental fall of a few 12-pounder shells would appear to be a minor matter.

But Major Hawkins, writing in the *Proceedings of the RA Institute* in 1912, was more concerned:

> A great disadvantage of shrapnel is the unavoidable return to earth of its bullets and pieces, a serious matter when we consider the number of shells that will certainly be necessary to get a hit, so that except in great emergency it will not be permissible to fire in directions that will damage our own troops. Moreover, officers and NCOs must have an instinctive acquaintance with the vertical trajectories of the guns so as to decide promptly whereabouts the debris will return to earth.

It is a comment upon the interpretation of the rules of war that both these gentlemen were concerned (or unconcerned) about the effect on their own *troops*. The idea that the civil population might be at risk from the falling debris appears not to have registered with them at that time, though (as we have seen) it later occurred to Major Hawkins when he suggested warning them not to venture out-of-doors when the guns were firing.

The army's other path of development took a curious turn, resulting in the 4-inch High Angle Mark 1, which was approved on New Year's Eve 1913. The design was much the same as that of the 3-inch 20cwt gun, so much so that it was decided to make the (then) naval 3-inch into a common service weapon, and the 4-inch was approved for Naval Service Only. The reasoning behind this decision is far from clear but it seems that the 4-inch weapon was considered more useful in a dual-purpose surface/air naval application than the 3-inch, since it could fire a more effective armour-piercing shell in the anti-ship role. Whatever the reason, the production of the gun was even slower than that of the 3-inch and by August 1914 only one was in use, firmly set in a concrete emplacement at Portsmouth Dockyard.

Guns, though, were relatively simple; carriages a trifle more difficult. Ammunition seemed to be straightforward but some practical trials would settle whether the explosive or the shrapnel shell was best or whether some new contender might be devised. The remaining problem was that of directing the gun so that the shell would hit the target. The problem was, in fact, threefold: firstly, to determine the range

to the target; secondly, to point the gun so that the shell would arrive somewhere near the target; and thirdly, to make accurate assessments of the errors involved when the shell burst and then to correct the fire until the target was hit. These three functions were the basics of all gunnery, and it seemed that the only logical answer must be to apply them to aircraft targets just as they were applied to land and sea targets. But there were some doubters. Lieutenant C. V. S. Skrimshire, RGA was one:

> At present [1913] no satisfactory anti-aircraft gun has been designed and, until an automatic sight is produced, the efforts of artillery to inflict damage . . . are unlikely to give adequate results. The impossibility of observing fire, even when the projectile is provided with a 'tracer' or device for following its flight, as well as the great difficulty of finding the range,

The British 4-inch High Angle gun was originally designed for the Army, but the Navy coveted it since it could fire a useful anti-ship shell and it eventually became a naval weapon.

make the problem one of unequalled difficulty. Many writers have advocated the use of specially constructed high-angle guns firing special ammunition . . . but nowhere has any real success been achieved. The rapidly varying height of the target, the quickly changing course as well as the high speed at which the aeroplane travels make it almost impossible to be anything but extremely doubtful of the utility of artillery fire.

The automatic sight, which Skrimshire was not the only person to demand, was a rangefinding sight used with coastal artillery guns. Each gun had a telescope sight mounting which contained a cam, carefully designed and shaped according to the height of the gun above the sea. Since this height was constant (except for tidal variations, for which a compensating device allowed) it formed the base of a right-angled triangle, the side of which was the surface of the sea and the hypotenuse the telescope's line of sight. Thus, for every range along the sea level there was a corresponding angle of depression of the telescope, and the shaped cam interacted with the gun's elevating gears so that when the crosswires of the telescope were laid on the waterline of a ship the gun was automatically given the correct elevation to hit the ship.

It can be appreciated from this brief description that adapting an autosight to an antiaircraft gun was almost impossible since one of the constants in the equation – the fact that the ship must be on the surface of the sea – was missing; the aircraft could be at any height. On the other hand, it shows the preoccupation with putting the sighting system on the gun – which, after all, was the traditional way of doing things – which bedevilled designers for a long time. Only the percipient Major Hawkins had discerned the correct solution, but nobody took him seriously.

> . . . the crux is the invention of an autosight . . .

If the apparatus were found to be too cumbersome to install on the mounting, it might be used separately, the gun being trained and elevated by electricity. The extra expense would be well repaid by increased accuracy over any other system.

Generally speaking the preferred solution seemed to be to lay down some simple rules that could be followed in the majority of cases, for as one critic put it:

> The use of delicate instruments entailing complicated calculations in the battlefield is quite out of place at present, and a few rough and ready rules which can easily be assimilated . . . could be far more effective in time of war than the use of any special instrument except perhaps a very rapidly acting one-man range-finder.

In this spirit the German Army instructed its infantry to fire from two to ten lengths ahead of an aircraft according to the estimated range; apparently the speed was considered to be more or less constant. The French School of Musketry produced a formidable set of rules which began: 'As soon as a flying machine is observed, judge its distance rapidly by eye or by telemeter [range-finder] and if the machine is not more than 25 degrees (the breadth of one hand) above the horizon, sight for the estimated distance less 200 metres and fire for thirty seconds,' and then got more and more involved as it attempted to cater for approaching, crossing or receding targets.

These rules were as good as could be hoped for with rifle fire, but artillery fire had to be rather more complex. In the absence of an accurate form of sighting system, most people fell back on approximations in the hope that if a great enough diversity of metal was flung into the sky then by the law of averages some of it ought to intercept the aircraft:

> Get a group of fuzed shells ready with the same length of fuze and fire them quickly . . .

Suppose the machine is sighted at 6,000 yards, travelling more or less towards the guns; the section commander orders ten rounds with 4,000 yards fuze, ten with 3,000, ten with 2,000. He opens fire when the range is 5,000 yards. As soon as a burst is observed close up, he comes down to the next group of fuzes.

Another suggestion was based on the French system of 'collective ranging' in which the range was estimated and each gun opened fire at a different fuze length and range so that the target would be bracketed. Having observed the distribution of these first shots and assessed which combination was most close to the target, the battery commander would then order a fuze and range at which all guns would open fire.

And, of course, the biggest problem of all was how were they to practise these theories? Even if they had some guns and some ammunition and some sights – which they hadn't – their only possible target was a kite towed behind a horse or a fast ship, and neither of those could reach the speed or altitude of an aircraft, be it airship or aeroplane. And quite obviously a real aeroplane or airship could not be used as a target. This was going to be the unique case of a system which could be theorized about as much as you liked in peacetime but which could only be practically evolved in war. What was needed was the war.

2 Archie and Friends

DEVELOPMENTS IN WORLD WAR ONE

At the outbreak of war in 1914 the entire world stock of anti-balloon guns could have been assembled on any convenient football field, with room to spare. And, since the various armies were more concerned with their mobilization and manoeuvring for position on either side of the German border, it might well have stayed that way for some time had it not been for Mr Winston Churchill. As First Lord of the Admiralty he was in a good position to make his wishes felt and when the Admiralty, as a body, decided that attack was the best form of defence, he ordered the Royal Naval Air Service to attack the German airship base at Düsseldorf. On 8 October 1914 Lieutenant Marix flew from an advanced base near Antwerp to Düsseldorf, dropped two 20lb bombs, scored two direct hits on the massive airship hangar and destroyed both the hanger and the Zeppelin inside it. Unfortunately, just as Marix returned from this epoch-making flight, the Germans advanced against Antwerp, the Naval airstrip had to be evacuated, and Düsseldorf was no longer within range of any available aircraft.

However, the raid had shown that aircraft were not going to be confined to reconnaissance roles as had been forecast, and that some form of active defence had to be looked to before this sort of thing became too common. The question then arose of what to use.

Britain had one 4-inch and four 3-inch AA guns in service; it also had a small stock of Maxim one-pounder 'Pom-Pom' guns, and so, as a first step, these were assembled either on pedestals in dockyard areas or on simple two-wheeled field carriages for issue to the army in Flanders.

The next approach was to see what guns, already in service or in reserve, could be modified to fire upwards with the least trouble. And here there was a stroke of luck. The war in Flanders was turning into a siege, with two trench lines extending from the North Sea to the Swiss frontier, conditions in which the light, short-range, highly mobile 13-pounder Royal Horse Artillery gun was of little use. So it was retired, the batteries being armed with 18-pounders as they became available. The 13-pounder was now contemplated as an anti-aircraft gun, and, it turned out, the shell had good ballistic qualities and a useful performance could be extracted from the gun – if it could be fitted to a suitable mounting.

At this time – late 1914 – the 'fire brigade' theory of air defence was still attractive. Put the gun on to a motor chassis so that it could be centrally based and then, on the approach of a target, it could drive out so as to position itself in the aircraft's path. If it missed, then after a furious drive it might be able to get into position for another few shots. So the 13-pounder gun was fitted to a relatively simple pedestal mount which was then bolted down to the cargo platform of any available motor truck, and the resulting equipment became the '13-pounder of 6-hundredweight' to distinguish it from the original '13-pounder Mark 1' and, with a slightly more powerful cartridge than used in the original horse artillery role, it was capable of firing its shrapnel shell to 5,000m (16,000ft) altitude. It was formally approved on 1 October 1914 and the first issues were sent out to the British Expeditionary Force in France in early December.

The 1-pounder Maxim Pom-Pom on its field carriage. Note the offset sights and the remote control, which allowed the sight setter to alter the lead setting without getting in the gunner's line of sight.

One of the few modifications to these guns necessary to turn them into anti-aircraft weapons was a 'Catch, Retaining Cartridge' which was fitted into the edge of the chamber so as to hold the loaded cartridge in place while the breech was closed with the gun at a high angle of elevation. Without this catch the loader would have had a tricky job trying to hold the round in the chamber whilst the breech operator tried to close the breech without removing the loader's fingers. After the war, those guns which had survived were dismounted from their trucks, replaced on their horse artillery carriages, and had the Catch, Retaining Cartridge removed. You may still see them from time to time: they are currently being used by the King's Troop RHA as saluting guns.

By January 1915 sufficient 13-pounder 6cwt guns had been produced to allow the formation of 'AA Sections', each of two guns, with

The 13-pounder High Angle Mark 1, which was the original RHA gun removed from its wheeled carriage and fitted to a simple pedestal mounting. A 'Catch, Retaining Cartridge' prevented the round from falling out when loaded at extreme elevations.

the intention of providing one such section to each division, but this aim was never reached. By July 1915 there were twenty-eight divisions in France but only thirteen AA Sections. Nevertheless, the guns did good work until that month, when they suddenly came under a cloud due to a change of ammunition policy. The shrapnel shell had several advantages as an anti-aircraft weapon, notably the spread of bullets, which considerably increased the chance of hitting. But it also suffered from one notable defect, which was that the shell's nose section, complete with fuze – weighing about 500g (1lb) – and the empty shell body – weighing about 3 kg (7lb) – fell back to earth after functioning in the sky, and in spite of Colonel Bethell's nonchalant dismissal of the problem in pre-war days, when it actually started to happen the luckless soldiers on the ground were not slow to complain. As a result the high-explosive shell was hurried into service; the detonation of an HE shell produced a shower of small fragments to rain down on the ground beneath, and this was considered to be

rather less hazardous than shrapnel-shell debris.

Unfortunately the manufacture of the early batches of high-explosive shells was hurriedly done and inspection of the finished product was cursory, due to the lack of experience in factories suddenly converted to munitions production. As a result, a large proportion of 13-pounder HE shells were 'high to gauge' or, in non-service English, too big to go up the gun's barrel; they jammed as they entered the rifling and this sudden check detonated the explosive inside, destroying the guns and killing or wounding the gunners. There was an understandable reluctance to fire the 13-pounder with high-explosive shells and huge amounts of ammunition had to be withdrawn for testing – this, on top of the general shortage of ammunition which obtained in 1915, severely curtailed the activities of the AA Sections and it was not until early in 1916 that confidence was restored with the regular issue of reliable ammunition.

On the other side of the front it seemed to the Allied aviators that, as usual, the Germans had

The Krupp 77mm 'Sockel-Flak' in action in 1915. One can see the beginnings of the outrigger platform, which became universal practice in later years. Another pair of wheels, probably off the picture to the left, would be required to lift everything off the ground for horse-transport.

better weapons, and they were not slow to complain about the power of the German guns. It was about this period that anti-aircraft guns collected the nickname that was to accompany them until 1939 – 'Archie'. The story goes that a young British pilot flying over the German lines used to express his disdain for the shells that burst around him by using the 'punch-line' from a music-hall song of the day; as his aircraft rocked to the blast, he would sing out 'Archibald – certainly NOT!'. The story got about, as such stories do, and before long all anti-aircraft guns were known as 'Archibald', shortened, in due course, to 'Archie'.

But in spite of the Allied pilots fears, the truth of the matter was that in August 1914 the Germans were little better off than anyone else in the matter of high-angle guns; they had six motorized guns, three by Krupp and three by Erhardt, all of which were actually the 1909 Frankfurt show models. There were also a dozen horse-drawn equipments, all of 77mm calibre, from various makers. Once war began, the motorized models were given 1,000 rounds of shrapnel each and sent to serve with the field armies. The horse-drawn weapons were dispersed along the Rhine valley, with 2,000 rounds apiece, placed so as to protect the major munitions installations such as the Krupp and Zeppelin factories.

Like the other combatants Germany was unprepared for the astonishing rate of attrition of weapons and equipment and the unparalleled demands for replacements and ammunition that resulted from modern warfare. Their reserves dwindled rapidly and their factories were slow to get into production with the replacement standard weapons, without even thinking about developing entirely new ones. So the first demands for anti-aircraft guns were met in a rather unusual way. In the first campaigns on the Eastern Front a large number of 76mm Russian field guns had been captured; these weapons, the Putilov M1903, had the unusually high muzzle velocity of 605m/sec (2,000ft/sec) and fired a useful 6.55kg (14lb) shrapnel shell. They were therefore converted to pedestal mounting as the *7.62cm Russische Sockellafette Fliegerabwehrkanone.* The latter part of the title, which literally meant 'flyer defence cannon', was soon abbreviated, in typical German fashion, to 'Flak', which has

remained the official German term ever since and, since World War Two, has been adopted as popular terminology, frequently misunderstood and often misspelt.

Subsequent German development followed two paths; the adaptation of existing field guns and the development of entirely new purpose-built AA guns. The latter path led slowly to a quite effective 88mm gun in 1918, which, though built by Krupp, bore no relationship other than its calibre to the more famous weapon by the same maker fielded in World War Two. But by far the greater proportion of the German defences, particularly in the fighting zones, was made up from conventional 77mm field guns of various models, with their axles lifted into the air on various types of staging so that the trails, remaining on the ground, allowed the guns to elevate to 70 degrees or so. The mounting was pivoted in one way or another so that all-round traverse was possible and, in spite of their extemporized air,

A Krupp 7.7cm field gun, converted into anti-aircraft, and mounted on a 'Pferdwagen' or horse-drawn platform.

Among the first of several 88mm designs from Krupp was this trailer-mounted model with a 45-calibre length gun.

The 88mm L/45 gun ready to move, behind its 100hp Daimler-Benz tractor.

An unidentified model of the 88mm gun behind a different type of tractor, which more resembles a gigantic touring car. Note the track-laying wheels for negotiating soft ground.

One of the most common German solutions to the anti-aircraft problem was to simply cobble together some sort of rotating stage capable of supporting a standard field gun. This is the 77mm Feldkanone 16nA on a mounting made from railway sleepers, timber and cartwheels.

An early German sound detector in use. With a single horn it could give some warning but very little directional information.

these guns appear to have served very satisfactorily throughout the war.

The French had, of course, approached the air defence problem in the same way that, at that time, they approached any artillery problem: they pointed their 75mm Gun Model of 1897 at it. The 75mm Mle 1897 was the all-purpose gun, it had good velocity and a 6kg (13lb) shell, and all that was necessary was to provide a suitable mounting. For the fixed defences around Paris and other major cities, a simple framework revolving around a pivot pin set in a stone foundation block was a crude but effective solution. For the field armies, where mobility was paramount, the '75mm Autocanon' was developed, a Panhard or De Dion Bouton touring-car chassis, with the rear section strengthened and fitted with a 75mm gun mounted on a rotating platform. A pair of stabilizing jacks held the rear end steady and relieved the springs of load when the gun fired,

the gun layers sat on the gun and attended to the arithmetic and the loaders stood on the ground and loaded. This became very popular, and, in due course, a number were acquired by Britain for use in the London defences.

But, soon realizing that the Autocanon was a rather expensive and luxurious solution, a towed two-wheeled mounting was developed, the ancestor of virtually all the 'platform and outrigger' types of anti-aircraft mounting that have followed. A small platform carried an axle with two wheels and had the gun mounted on a turntable; at each corner was a curved outrigger that could be swung down and then, by means of screw jacks, forced down so as to lift the wheels clear of the ground. As with the Autocanon, the gun layers sat on the mounting and revolved with the gun, while the ammunition handlers ran around following the breech.

In Britain the next stage of gun provision was to ask the gun makers to turn out their stock

The Germans were not alone in inventing extemporized gun mountings. This was the French solution to the problem: put the standard 75mm Mle 1897 field gun on to a framework of angle iron and put it on a pivot in a pit.

The other side of the French 75 mounting.

The other French solution was undoubtedly the most elegant of the wartime self-propelled machines – the 75mm Autocanon.

cupboards and see what they had. In the spring of 1915 much of this stock was acquired by the Army and Royal Navy, and some odd things came to light. The Elswick Ordnance Company, for example, had a variety of 3-inch guns intended for foreign contracts. Six of these resembled the 13-pounder 6cwt but were shorter and were rifled with twenty-four grooves instead of the eighteen grooves of the service pattern; these were mounted on motor chassis and taken for Army use, one going to guard the Royal Small Arms Factory at Enfield Lock and the other five to France, being officially known as the '13-pounder Mark IV'. Another design, again similar to the 13-pounder 6cwt but with a much different breech mechanism, became the '3-inch 5cwt' and four were taken for protection of dockyards. Elswick appeared to have had some stock of components for these weapons since another eight were then built and, mounted on lorries, went to swell the AA Sections in France.

A third Elswick gun was one that had been designed for the Russian Navy; it was a 75mm weapon firing a 4.85kg (11lb) shell and was on a high-angle mounting. Twelve of these were taken by the Royal Navy and known as the '10-pounder Russians', but the complication of having to organize a special ammunition supply for the ships which would carry them was more than they were worth and they were eventually given to the Army to be used in the London defences, the Navy taking a dozen new 3-inch 20cwt guns in their place.

These were, of course, stop-gap weapons and were never considered for formal adoption and further manufacture because, while they could undoubtedly shoot upwards, they were far from being the best possible design. For the next 'regulation' gun the solution seemed fairly obvious; if the 3-inch calibre 13-pounder was good, then the 3.3-inch calibre 18-pounder would be better. So the same conversion was tried with the Royal Field Artillery's 18-pounder. But the 18-pounder

The 75mm Autocanon in the firing position. Note the stabilizing jacks, and also the enormously complicated sights required when all the fire control calculation was done on the gun.

proved to be useless as an anti-aircraft gun; for a variety of technical ballistic reasons the 18-pounder shell did not perform well in high-angle fire and the project had to be abandoned. In August 1915, however, the Director of Artillery suggested putting a 3-inch calibre liner into the barrel of the 18-pounder so that the resulting weapon would use the 18-pounder cartridge to fire the 13-pounder shell. Within a week the idea

had been examined, tried and pronounced workable, and fifty 18-pounders were relined, placed on modified 13-pounder pedestals and fitted to Peerless motor trucks. This new weapon had a muzzle velocity of 655m/sec (2,150ft/sec) and a ceiling of 5,800m (19,000ft), and in order to avoid confusion it became known as the '13-pounder 9cwt'. The first equipments were issued in November 1915 and in due course it replaced

The French 75mm 'remorque' mounting, in action. The three men are all laying or setting the sights, and another two on the other side were similarly occupied. The actual loading and firing was done from the ground.

all the older 13-pounder models in France; the French army were sufficiently impressed with it to ask for thirty guns for use in their own rear areas.

The system that had gradually evolved in France was to establish a line of AA sections some 3–4,000 yards (2.5–3.5km) behind the trenches; by late 1915 there were sufficient weapons to provide one section for every 4 miles (6.5km) of front. The sections prepared a number of sites in their area, and they would drive forward and occupy one of these sites shortly before dawn. As targets appeared, so they would be engaged, but sooner or later the German aviators complained, on their return home, and the location of the offending 'Archie' would be passed to the German field artillery for counter-bombardment. Since the 'Archie' was motorized, as soon as the first ranging round landed it was time to wind up the jacks, swing in the stabilizing outriggers, crank up the

engine and depart to another of the prepared positions.

As darkness fell, flying activity usually ceased and the 'Archie' and its crew would then drive back to their billets some 3,000 yards (2.5km) further back, and settle down for the night. The guns were placed 'in action' in case a night flyer chanced along and, as the war progressed and night flying became more common, searchlight sections were deployed and a second line of AA Sections was dispersed further back, among the railheads, supply dumps and base areas.

While the supply organizations were worrying about guns and ammunition, the men on the ground were worrying about the more pressing problem of how to hit the target. The science of anti-aircraft gunnery was being worked out from first principles over the Western Front, by a system of trial and error. Shooting was done entirely by eye and the techniques employed were simply extensions of the methods of fire

The British 13-pounder Mark 4 was a non-standard gun intended for the export market, but it fired the standard ammunition, so that was all right.

The '10-pounder Russian' started life as a dual-purpose gun for the Russian Navy. The last dozen, undelivered on the outbreak of war, were commandeered by the Royal Navy but their demand for special ammunition made life too complicated and they were off-loaded onto the army.

The 13-pounder 9cwt was an 18-pounder gun sleeved down to 13-pounder calibre, but still using the 18-pounder cartridge. It became the mainstay of the British field army AA artillery and remained in use in some countries until the early 1930s.

correction used by field and garrison artillery against terrestrial targets. An aircraft would be seen approaching; its range would be measured by an optical range-finder, typically the two-metre-base Barr and Stroud; the height had to be estimated, and from this height and range a fuze-length was determined for the setting of the shell's time fuze. This was, of course, calculated (by means of a graphical chart) for the future position of the aircraft, the position it was assumed it would be occupying when the shell finally got there, some thirty seconds or so after being fired. Suitable deflections were calculated – or guessed – and set on to the gun's sight, so that when the gun layer pointed the

sight at the aircraft, the gun's muzzle would be pointed at the future position. And finally the shell was loaded and the gun was fired.

In terrestrial gunnery practice there would now be a pause until the shell arrived and burst, after which a correction would be deduced from the relative positions of shell and target and a fresh round fired. But with the target soaring across the sky at speed, such leisurely methods could no longer be used, and the gun continued to fire, as fast as it could, using the same initial information. After five or six shots had gone, the first would burst in the sky and the observing officer could then make an estimate of the error, recalculate his data, and give fresh orders to the gun. Obviously, there were defects in this system. The initial data were largely based on guesswork, while the subsequent corrections were all based on out-of-date information.

The first improvement was to modify the range-finder so that it also measured the vertical angle to the target and thus allowed the height to be calculated with some accuracy. Next came the Wilson-Dalby Deflection Meter, a telescope controlled by a geared handle. An observer, looking through the telescope, tracked the target in flight by turning the handle; this allowed the rate of movement of the aircraft to be mechanically measured, and this rate, together with the known range and height, enabled an accurate deflection to be calculated. The process was speeded up by fitting scales to the gun sight matching the readings from the deflection meter. The correct deflection was automatically worked out and set into the sight without the need to calculate it, but since the gun layer wanted to keep his eye on the target, another man had to be drafted in to set the deflection on the sight. A further improvement came with a French invention, the Brocq Tachymeter, which did the same job, but did it electrically instead of mechanically and displayed the correct deflection on a dial attached to the gun; in this case the calculation was

An AA Section in France, 1918, with their 13-pounder 9cwt guns.

13-pounder Mark 1 guns firing at night in France, 1916.

A rare bird which was never on the approved list: the 12-pounder 12cwt coast-defence gun adapted to the anti-aircraft role. A number were tried but they were ballistically unsatisfactory and the experiment was discontinued.

The 12-pounder on a mobile carriage; it was no more successful than the static design and few were ever made.

An unexplained photograph found in an old archive and entitled '18-pounder with A.A. Apparatus'. Not the least interesting feature of this picture is that the gun carriage is anchored to a ground platform, in the same manner as the much later 25-pounder gun.

performed electrically inside the tachymeter, which simplified the design of the gun sight.

By this time the aviators had discovered that flying below 1,000m (3,000ft) was distinctly hazardous due to rifle and machine-gun fire from the trenches; above 1,000m this was of no account, and it was the fire of the anti-aircraft guns which mattered, so it became their practice to fly at 3,000 to 3,500m (10,000 to 12,000ft) and thus avoid all danger from the ground. But as the gunnery improved, so the dangerous height crept upward and the aviators moved up to 4,500m (15,000ft) or so.

This was satisfactory for a while and then the danger height climbed again and the aviators went up to 6,000m (20,000ft). So far the guns had justified their existence; as a prominent French anti-aircraft gunner, Colonel Pagezy, said: 'The function of anti-aircraft guns is to punish the audacity of aircraft flying in a straight line, hinder and obstruct others in the performance of their duties, and prevent aeroplanes flying at low heights.' And this had been done. However, once the targets were higher than 4,500m the accuracy of artillery fire sud-

American gunners using a Brocq Tachymeter.

denly became most erratic, and it was obvious that some fundamental research had to be done.

The problem was how to find a system of actually measuring the gun's performance; the only way to do this was to be able to locate the shell burst in the sky with great precision, so that the result of corrections or experiments could be accurately measured. After many false starts this problem was solved by Major A. V. Hill (later to be better known as Professor A. V. Hill, FRS) and Sir Horace Darwin, who, in early 1916, invented the Mirror Position Finder. This was an optically flat and carefully levelled mirror some 30in (76cm) square, laid flat so as to reflect the sky. Two observers watched the surface of the mirror through fixed peep-sights and, upon seeing the reflection of a shell-burst, marked its apparent position on the mirror's surface. From this, by some fairly abstruse geometry and mathematics, it was possible to deduce the position of the burst in the sky with remarkable accuracy.

With the mirror position finder to give the basic facts, the Ministry of Munitions set up an Anti-Aircraft Experimental Section at Portsmouth, using the gun-firing facilities of Whale Island, the RN Gunnery School, and systematic testing of every aspect of the anti-aircraft system got under way. It soon became apparent that the prime cause of trouble lay in the time fuzes. The fuzes in use at this time were operated by the burning of a train of gunpowder. As the gun was fired an igniting detonator in the fuze struck a fixed needle; the resulting flash lit the end of the powder train, which then began to burn at a speed predetermined by the composition of the powder and the density with which it was packed. But it was now apparent that something was upsetting the regularity of the powder at heights over 4,500m. The AAES built a vacuum chamber and installed a spinning table inside it so that the fuze could be operated in conditions of spin and rarefied atmosphere exactly like those it would meet in the air when fired. These experiments showed

that the burning powder was often extinguished due to the drop in air pressure at great heights. Another defect was the centrifugal force due to the spinning shell, which caused the molten, burning area of the powder to detach itself from the rest of the train and thus fail to pass on the ignition. By reformulating the powder and changing the internal arrangements in the fuzes, they were gradually made more reliable, but even when the war ended 6,000m (20,000ft) seemed to be the greatest height at which a combustion fuze could be relied upon to function with any degree of accuracy.

Besides the actual question of shooting at aircraft there was also the question of detecting them; the sooner the target was detected, the more time there would be in which to calculate the initial data and the sooner the shooting could start. The only detection method, at first, was the human eye, but this was a highly variable system; two men with identical vision could differ widely in their ability to spot and follow an aircraft. The average aeroplane of the day, it was calculated, occupied about one twenty-millionth part of the sky, and in some conditions of lighting could be virtually invisible at ranges as short as 5,000 metres (3 miles).

Apart from vision, the only other detectable feature of the aeroplane was its noise, and in 1915 the first primitive sound detector was produced by the London air defences. This consisted of a long pole, mounted so as to rotate horizontally on a pivot, and bearing at each end a gramophone horn. Attached to the horns were rubber tubes that led in to the centre of the pole and terminated in a pair of stethoscope earpieces. The operator placed these in his ears, and by this actually extended the 'base' of his two ears, so that by turning the pole about its pivot until the sound of the aircraft could be heard equally in each ear, he could determine the direction from which the sound was coming. To try to extract the utmost from this idea, blind men were used as operators in some instances, on the premise that a man born blind would have a more highly developed sense of hearing than a man who relied principally on his eyesight. It appears to have worked well, but there were practical difficulties in the supply of suitable blind men, and, moreover, the system could hardly have been exported to the battle lines in France.

Sound detectors of more elegant patterns followed, and a vertically mounted pair of horns allowed an estimation of height to be made. Eventually a four-horn unit was evolved in which the two horns in the horizontal plane gave direction and one horizontal horn with others above and below it gave height, two operators being used. In still air, with no other noises to distract the operators, these devices could pick up an approaching aircraft at about 5 miles range (8km), which wasn't a lot better than a good visual observer, but it could continue to do it in cloudy or hazy conditions that defeated the human eye. The French Army developed a much more sophisticated device in which a large parabolic reflector collected the sound and concentrated it into an electrical microphone at the reflector's focal point from where it was relayed to the operator's earphones. By careful manipulation of the reflector, moving it until the sound was at its loudest, accuracy in azimuth and elevation of about 3 degrees was possible. But, as already discussed, ranging on a moving object by sound is a deceptive business since the target can get up to all sorts of tricks while the sound is travelling towards the detector. And with a maximum sound detection range of about five or six miles in those pre-amplification days, and with aircraft increasing in speed with every new model that appeared, the early warning was getting later and later.

Another thing which made itself apparent was that the time-honoured system of building an expensive and complicated sight for the gun and feeding it with all the available information for it to mechanically sort out and set an eleva-

The perfection of World War One design – the 3-inch 20cwt on Peerless Lorry mounting.

tion and deflection, was not the way to go. Two layers were required for each gun, one for line, one for elevation, and since they were totally absorbed in peering through their telescopes and tracking the target, they could not stop this activity to re-set sights with fresh data every few minutes; so they were each provided with a sight-setter whose sole job was to set pointers and twist knobs, applying the various corrections, whereupon the cursing gun layers would wind their handles furiously in order to get their cross wires back to their target before they lost it completely. Not the least of the defects with this system was the demand for four highly trained specialists for every gun.

With the Wilson-Dalby and Brocq instruments, and a few additions such as the range/height finder and sundry graphical calculators, the 'Central Post System' was gradually evolved. Now the tracking was done by a single instrument in the centre of the gun group, a future position was calculated, fuze length, elevation and azimuth to it were determined and the result given to the guns. They simply set their elevation and traverse scales at the figures ordered, set the fuzes to the length ordered, loaded and fired as fast as they could. And with the sight-setters cleared away from the gun platform there was more room for the loaders and the rate of fire generally improved.

By the middle of the war, therefore, the anti-aircraft tactics on the Western Front had become fairly standardized on both sides of the line. Each side spread two rows of guns behind the trench line, as thickly as they could afford, and shot at anything approaching from the other side. On top of that the French and Germans also dispersed whatever guns they could spare around the major towns and cities behind the line, though, of course, this was tempered by an appreciation of the capabilities of the aircraft of the day. The French put guns around Paris because it was no more than half an hour's flying time from the front; the Germans did not put guns around Berlin

because no aircraft could have reached it and returned to the Allied side of the lines. Moreover the Allies did not have any long-range aircraft with which to engage in long-range raiding, while the Germans had the Zeppelin airships. The Germans also had the Schutte-Lanz and Parseval airships, but it is the Zeppelin that has gone down in history as the major air threat. And the Zeppelin threat was the motor that drove the air defences of Britain for most of the war.

THE DEFENCE OF LONDON

England's air space was finally invaded on 21 December 1914 when a German aircraft appeared over Dover, dropped two bombs into the harbour close to the Admiralty Pier, then turned about and flew back to its base in Belgium. Three days later another aircraft ventured slightly further, to drop a bomb close to Dover castle. And finally, on Christmas Day, a German Albatros seaplane flew up the Thames estuary. A gun in Sheerness Dockyard fired at it as it passed; three aircraft of the Royal Flying Corps took off in pursuit from Eastchurch, on the Isle of Sheppey, and caught up with the intruder at Erith. Whereupon the Albatros turned round and raced back down the estuary for home. As it passed Cliffe Fort another gun opened fire, at which the pilot took exception and dropped a bomb, narrowly missing Cliffe railway station, before flying off unscathed.

Eventually, of course, this comic opera style of warfare ceased and the serious threat made itself apparent. On 19 January 1915 three German Naval airships, L3, L4 and L6 set out across the North Sea to see what they could find. L6 developed engine trouble halfway across the sea and turned back. L3 and L4 reached the coast of Norfolk, where L3 turned to Great Yarmouth and dropped nine bombs, while L4 turned north, dropping a few bombs at random as it passed over various villages. By

French troops firing a captured Maxim one-pounder gun.

that time night had fallen and the Zeppelin commander, Kapitänleutnant Graf von Platen, seeing lights beneath him and believing he had reached the Humber estuary, dropped all his bombs hoping to hit some of the Humberside industrial establishments. Map-reading was obviously not one of von Platen's strong points. The bombs landed on King's Lynn, killing two and injuring thirteen people.

Reading contemporary reports, one gets the impression that the over-riding feeling among the English was not anger or hatred but indignation; how *dare* these wretched Germans do such a thing! This was quickly followed by a clamour for defensive guns to be thickly sown across Britain. In January 1915 the only guns deployed, as we have seen, were about half-a-dozen of major calibre and about two-dozen

Stolen fruit always tastes sweeter; Russian troops firing a captured Austrian Schwarzlose machine gun at Austrian aircraft.

Pom-Poms around London, so there was not much chance of thickening the defences of East Anglia or anywhere else. But so that Something Would Be Seen To Be Done, the 'Eastern Mobile Air Defence Force' was hastily assembled, a collection of Vickers machine guns and searchlights mounted on motor trucks and stationed at Newmarket. Local policemen all over the eastern counties were provided with the telephone number of the Force HQ, and should they see a Zeppelin approaching they were to telephone the Force, which would then turn out and Do Something. In order that the other side of London should not feel neglected, a Southern Mobile Force was assembled at Caterham but, since this avenue of approach was never used by the Germans, they were disbanded some months later.

By this time, too, some degree of information had been gathered about where the German machines were based and, in a praiseworthy attempt to combine protection with economy, three 3-inch guns, wheedled from the Royal Navy's allocation, were installed around London in carefully selected positions. One gun was placed on Clapton Orient's football ground, for this lay on a line between central London and the Zeppelin bases at Nordholz and Tondern. The second gun was emplaced at One Tree Hill (Honour Oak Park) on a line to the Belgian bases at Gontrode and Otterbeek; while the third was on Parliament Hill, Hampstead Heath, where it could provide some protection for the north-western suburbs.

The next Zeppelin attack was a more casual affair. Zeppelin L9 was on a reconnaissance flight across the North Sea to see what there was to be seen in the north-east of England. It had some bombs on board; the weather was fine; the airship running smoothly; so the commander decided to turn inland and make a nuisance of himself. Crossing the coast at Blyth he was peppered with rifle fire by a Cyclists' Battalion of Militia on their summer camp, but apart from that he met no resistance. Once again darkness overtook the Zeppelin and, by this time, lighting restrictions were being enforced on Tyneside, so the commander was unable to pick up anything he could recognize to get his bearings. As a result, when he thought he was sailing down the Tyne scattering his bombs on to shipyards and engineering works, he was actually flying at right angles and bombing mostly empty farmland, only one bomb landing in a populated area in Wallsend. He then sailed off back to his base and reported on his adventures, which encouraged others to try their luck across the sea.

London's first Zeppelin attack was conducted by Hauptmann Linnarz in Zeppelin LZ38 on 31 May 1915. He approached London across Essex and dropped bombs in Stoke Newington, Stepney, Poplar, West Ham and Leytonstone, a total of some thirty explosive and ninety incendiary bombs. The Zeppelin flew high and was quite unseen from the ground; not surprisingly, no guns opened fire, and the raider went back the way he had come, leaving seven killed, thirty-five injured, and an estimated £18,000 worth of damage. This scot-free run caused some discontent and on 15 June the Admiralty reluctantly agreed to release another three 3-inch guns from the Fleet's store, siting them at Blackheath, Finsbury and West Ham.

Until now Kaiser Wilhelm had forbidden any raids on London west of the Tower, but on 18 June the German Admiralty (who were operating the airships at that time, since the army ships were not ready) requested permission to abandon this restriction, pointing out that virtually all the worthwhile targets – the War Office, Parliament, the banks – were in the west, and after some discussion they obtained permission on 20 June, on condition that historic buildings were not damaged. In August several naval airship raids were mounted, but for various reasons, generally connected with ill winds or poor navigation, few of them achieved any results and none of them managed to get near London. It was not until 17 August that Zeppelin L10 reached the capital, arriving over Walthamstow late at night to drop three bombs. It then flew on to Leyton to drop another twenty-six bombs, Leytonstone (four bombs), Wanstead (ten bombs) and then departed. A Pom-Pom at Waltham Abbey (defending the Royal Gunpowder Factory) managed to get off a few shots as the Zeppelin passed over on its way in to London, but no other guns saw it, nor did four aircraft which hunted for it across Essex.

On 7 September the German Army Airship Service appeared, intent upon bettering the Navy's achievements. SL2 (a Schutte-Lanz airship, not a Zeppelin) bombed Leytonstone again, flew on to Milwall, Deptford, Southwark, New Cross, Greenwich, Charlton and Woolwich, scattering bombs as it went, to kill eighteen and injure thirty-eight.

At the same time Zeppelin LZ74 approached down the Lea Valley, bombing Cheshunt as it passed; it was fired at by the Waltham Abbey gun (which appears to have had an alert detachment) and arrived over Fenchurch Street just after midnight. It dropped one incendiary bomb that did little damage but which went on record as being the first enemy missile to land within the City of London.

After this gesture, LZ74 joined up with SL2 and the pair flew off in company, both being fired at by the guns at Purfleet as they passed. Blowing out acres of greenhouses at Cheshunt in order to drop one ineffectual bomb on the City and scatter a few more on the inner suburbs scarcely made tactical sense, and perhaps somebody in Germany thought so too; in any event, it was the last time a German Army airship attacked London.

The Navy, however, were convinced that bombing could be made effective, and they proved their contention with their next raid, which took place on the following day. Zeppelin L13 crossed the Wash and made for London, passing over Cambridge en route. At 10.40pm it bombed Golders Green and then passed over Euston Station, Hatton Garden, Smithfield Market, Moorgate and Liverpool Street bombing as it went; twenty-two people were killed and eighty-seven injured, while property damage was estimated at over half a million pounds. All the London guns – by now twenty-six in number – opened fire without success, though they drove L13 up to 3,300m (11,000ft) altitude in order to escape the shells.

As might be imagined, the ability of the Zeppelins to sail in, bomb and sail out again without, apparently, much opposition, caused uproar in London. The Admiralty, who had been given responsibility for the air defence of Britain, decided, therefore, to divorce the London defences from the rest of Britain, put a strong man in charge and give him his head, and they appointed Admiral Sir Percy Scott, the renowned gunnery expert, to the job.

Scott's first move was to order the removal of the 1-pounder Pom-Poms as being useless and dangerous. He then demanded another 104 guns and fifty searchlights and, although a

Admiral Sir Percy Scott with, on the right, Commander Rawlinson and on the left the Grand Duke Michael of Russia at Kenwood House, Hampstead, then the HQ of the Royal Naval Air Service Anti-Aircraft Brigade.

gunnery specialist, he appreciated the part that aircraft could play. His plan of defence was to put the guns and the aircraft well forward so as to prevent an enemy from reaching London, reserving sufficient guns around the capital to deal with any which might get through; his view was that 'the defence of London by aircraft begins over the Zeppelin sheds and the defence by gunfire begins at the coast'.

This looked like being a fine start but, of course, he had no hope of receiving 104 guns; although he might have been able to obtain a few searchlights, since they were commonly used by the Navy and by the coast defences.

Scott decided that high-explosive shells were the correct projectile, but at that time there was no suitable time fuze, since time-fuzed HE shell had never been considered in field or coast defences. A fuze had been developed, but pro-

duction had yet to commence, and a suitable shell had to be designed. So Scott sent his deputy, Commander Rawlinson, post-haste to Paris to borrow one of the latest French AA guns and bring it back to England to be copied. This was the 75mm Autocanon, which was provided with a high explosive shell.

Rawlinson returned with number of Autocanon and, using this as a pattern, De Dion, Lancia and Daimler chassis were converted to carry mountings for a variety of British guns. The object of all this was to have a mobile column of guns that could be stationed centrally and, upon receipt of a warning of the approach of Zeppelins, could drive out rapidly and position itself across the raider's path to reinforce the static guns in the area. Vickers produced a supply of high-velocity 3-pounder guns suitable for mounting on lorry chassis and the

Coventry Ordnance Works undertook to build duplicates of the French Autocanon mounting, for which the French Government would supply the guns and ammunition. The 75mm Autocanons fired high explosive, the remainder fired shrapnel until HE shells became available, and the entire circus was stationed at Hampstead in north London.

The final raid of 1915 occurred on 15 October, when five airships set out and were spotted by a naval patrol vessel as they flew across the North Sea, and a radio message alerted the defences. On reaching the Norfolk coast, two airships swung west and set off for the Midlands to see what they could find. In the event they did very little damage and eventually went home. The other three turned south for London; L15 was the first to be seen, passing

over a gun site close to Broxbourne and being fired on. It dropped three bombs, narrowly missing the offending gun, passed over Edgware and into Central London, scattering some thirty bombs between Charing Cross and Limehouse. During this period it was illuminated by searchlights and every available gun fired at it, without any effect, and it eventually sailed off across Suffolk to the North Sea and home.

The second airship, L14, now appeared from the south; the captain had passed to the west of London unseen, swung round over Croydon and there dropped his bombs. Finally L13 appeared over Woolwich Arsenal and showered it with five HE and twenty-eight incendiary bombs, which did surprisingly little damage. Both L13 and L14 were also illuminated and

Admiral Scott and his entourage inspecting the guns at Kenwood House in 1916.

The Zeppelins didn't always get away with it; the L15 suffered gunfire damage on 1 April 1916, broke its back and crashed into the English Channel.

fired on, with no results, and the damage the three machines had done amounted to forty-one killed, eighty-five injured and considerable damage to property.

In September, Admiral Scott had asked for a further 100 fighter aircraft to be stationed around London and the south-eastern counties. With sufficient aircraft aloft, no Zeppelin ought to get as far as London, but in case any did, the gun strength would be increased to catch them. But 100 aircraft was beyond the capacity of the Royal Naval Air Service and would necessitate the Royal Flying Corps increasing its strength. This, of course, was a golden opportunity for the RFC to expand and the Army was quick to point out that if they were given the 100 aircraft and the men to operate them, they would be happy to take over the burden of air defence from the Navy, as had always been intended.

In February 1916, therefore, the responsibility for AA defence passed entirely into the hands of the War Office, and their Home Defence Directorate unveiled a scheme that they had prepared in anticipation of this handover. This divided the country into a number of primary areas that had to be defended because of the targets within them, plus a number of ports and scattered munitions factories outside the defined areas. The distribution of guns was to be such that a raider would meet an increasing volume of fire as he approached the centre of any area. Mobile gun sections would also be deployed, their positions being changed frequently so as to exploit the possibility of surprising a raider who thought he knew where the defences were. In the defence of London Sir Percy Scott's proposals were accepted and expanded, resulting in a double circle of guns around London, 5 and 9 miles from Charing Cross, with slight distortions to the outer circle to take in Woolwich Arsenal, the Royal Small Arms Factory, Enfield, and the Royal Gunpowder Factory, Waltham Abbey.

Outside the gun rings was an outer search-light ring, primarily intended to guide defending aircraft by signalling, with the beam, in the direction of any reported raider. The whole scheme demanded 475 guns and 500 searchlights; when the War Office took control they found themselves in possession of 295 guns in the whole of the United Kingdom, of which fifty-three were one-pounder Pom-Poms (which Scott had been unable to get rid of), 140 were 6-pounder Hotchkiss guns, twenty were 3-pounder Hotchkiss, and two were Naval 2-pounder Pom-Poms; none of this collection were considered to be of any operational value whatever. In the course of being transferred from naval stocks were another eighty guns which Scott had organized, but these turned out to be a collection of boneyard relics including four 6-inch guns on railway wagons, ten 4.7-inch ex-naval guns, twenty-eight French 75mm guns – some on Autocanon mounts and some on peculiar extemporized ground mounts – and, of course, the ubiquitous 10-pounder Russians still looking for a home. The Admiralty had also promised another eighty-six guns and it is interesting to speculate on what they might have been, but in the event, most of these failed to appear since they were suddenly needed 'to arm merchant ships against U-Boats' – which says a lot for their anti-aircraft potential.

So far the defence by aircraft had not been very successful, the principal reasons being that the available machines had no suitable ammunition with which to engage the targets and the pilots were quite inexperienced in night flying. The principal armament for the flyers at the end of 1915 was the Ranken Explosive Dart, or the 16lb Cooper bomb, both of which were supposed to be dropped from above so as to explode in contact with the airship frame, thus puncturing and igniting the gasbags. The machine gun appeared to be useless, since it merely punched small holes in the gasbags, never sufficiently serious to cause the airship to lose much height, and, being inert bullets, they failed to ignite the hydrogen.

Ever since the start of the war a Mr J. F. Buckingham, a Coventry engineer, had been working on the design of an incendiary bullet to defeat airships, a bullet that used a filling of phosphorus as the active agent. In late 1915 his design was perfected and issues began. It was followed by a design of tracer bullet developed by the Royal Laboratory at Woolwich Arsenal and subsequently manufactured in a factory owned by Messrs Aerators Ltd, from which the bullet acquired its name the 'Sparklet' bullet. Primarily intended to give aerial gunners an indication of the track their bullets were taking, these also had a slight incendiary effect. A third design came from Commander Brock of the Brock fireworks family, a bullet which was intended to explode after passing through the outer skin of the Zeppelin and thus attack the gasbags. Finally came the Pomeroy bullet, an ordinary 0.303 bullet with a tiny copper tube containing detonating composition inserted into the nose.

By mid-1916 most of these were in production, Lewis machine guns were carried on aircraft, and the days of the Zeppelin were numbered. The Lewis-gun drum was loaded with a combination of bullet types so that the Sparklet indicated the trajectory, the Brock blew a hole in the fabric, and the Buckingham and Pomeroy bullets ignited the escaping hydrogen. Using this combination Lieutenant Leefe Robinson shot down the Schutte-Lanz airship SL11 near Cuffley on 3 September 1916, for which he received the Victoria Cross. A few days later Second Lieutenant Alfred de Bath Brandon (RFC Special Reserve) shot at L33 but failed to ignite the gas. However, the airship commander decided that return to Germany was impossible and force landed the Zeppelin in Essex. For this Brandon added the DSO to his decorations. And on that same night Second Lieutenant F. Sowrey caught L32, 'hosed it with a stream of fire', to quote one eyewitness, and brought it down in flames close to Billericay.

In January 1917, confident that the defences now had the measure of the Zeppelin, a reduction in the strength of those defences was proposed. The history of anti-aircraft defence, anywhere and at any time, shows that it never pays to become too efficient, or somebody will inevitably tamper with the winning combination. This time it was the Admiralty demanding a proportion of the gun production earmarked for the air defences so that they could be used to arm more merchant ships against U-Boat attacks. The number of guns then allotted to London was eighty-four; this was now reduced to sixty-five. By February the strength stood at forty-eight 3-inch, sixteen 75mm mobile and static, one 12-pounder and one 3.5-inch (an odd weapon which appears in no artillery records and may have been an French 90mm gun on loan for trial purposes). In similar manner, the aircraft strength was reduced by sending two squadrons to France.

The sudden spate of destruction convinced the Germans that the Zeppelin was no longer a viable weapon system, and they mounted very few raids before the final one took place in October 1917. But by 1917 they had perfected the Zeppelin's replacement, and this was about to be unveiled.

On 25 May sixteen twin-engined Gotha biplane bombers appeared over the Essex coast, turned south because London was obscured by heavy cloud, and bombed Folkestone and Shornecliffe with heavy loss of life. While this was still being discussed and argued about, on 13 June a squadron of fourteen Gothas flew up the Thames in broad daylight and bombed Eltham, the Royal Albert Docks, Liverpool Street Station, Southwark and Dalston. A total of 162 people were killed and 432 injured in this brief raid. Ninety-two pilots took to the air but few saw the raiders and fewer still came within range of them; the raiders escaped unhurt.

Predictably, this raid set the country in an uproar. Plans were put forward for increasing the strength of the Royal Flying Corps, but little concrete action was taken other than to shuffle some of the guns around to give better protection to the eastern approaches to London. Before much else had been done the Gothas returned on 7 July, twenty-one aircraft flying across the East End and the City, bombing as they went. Fifty-four people were killed and 190 injured. Again, ninety-five pilots in twenty-one different kinds of aeroplane took to the air, but only one Gotha was shot down and that almost accidentally; it was found limping along the coast near the North Foreland and was shot into the sea by an aircraft of 50 Home Defence Squadron, a formation which was not, in fact, concerned with the defence of London at all.

This second daylight assault provoked an even greater public uproar. The War Cabinet met immediately and demanded the return of the two squadrons of aircraft from France. General Haig, predictably, protested that the whole of the Western Front would collapse about his ears, the request was halved and one squadron was returned, while another that had been about to leave for France was diverted to home defence. The next response of the War Cabinet was equally predictable; they set up a committee to look into the matter.

And just this once, this stereotyped response was probably the best thing they could have done, since the 'committee' virtually finished up as a one-man show in the person of Lieutenant General J. C. Smuts, a remarkable man by anybody's standards. Smuts had a legal background and could assimilate detail and convert it into simple statements. He actually produced two reports; his first dealt with the air defences, whilst his second dealt with the reorganization of the air forces.

Action followed rapidly. Brigadier General E. B. Ashmore was brought home from France to become the head of a new London Air Defence Area (LADA). Ashmore viewed his new appointment with a wry sense of humour; in his memoirs he observed that: 'We of the Expeditionary Force were inclined to look on the troubles of London somewhat light-heartedly. The fact that I was exchanging the comparative safety of the front for the probability of being hanged in the streets of London did not worry me.' Ashmore's first step was to set up a barrier line of guns some 32km (20 miles) out of London to the east. Moving the guns out to this distance meant that the fighters had a free hand on both sides of the gun line; they could, if they could find them, attack raiders coming over the coast, while other fighters on patrol behind the gun line would be able to pick off the Gothas one by one as their formations were broken up by gunfire. Searchlights and gun sites were provided with large moveable arrows, easily visible from the air, which were to be pointed towards any enemy aircraft in sight. This took advantage of the superior visibility of the ground observers over that of the pilots and ensured that fighters could be steered in the right direction.

To make sure that there would be fighters, three new squadrons were formed, and additional Home Defence Squadrons in Essex and Sussex were nominated as part of the London force and placed at Ashmore's disposal. A final innovation was to detail a number of wireless-equipped aircraft as 'trackers' whose sole task was to keep on the trail of the raiders and wireless their position and course back to the ground at intervals.

Lieutenant Colonel Simon, RE, who was the AA Defence Commander, London, had, on 21 June, put forward a scheme of improvement involving forty-five more guns on the outskirts so as to present an enemy with a barrier of shells, but this had been turned down. On 16 July he put forward another scheme for locating a ring of guns on a 25 mile (40km) radius from Charing Cross to break up enemy formations and allow the fighters to deal with them more easily. Lord French, Commander-in-Chief, endorsed this scheme and pressed it strongly to the War Cabinet, requesting 110 additional guns, but the Cabinet replied that the flow of

guns to the Merchant Navy could not be impeded, and if French wanted guns he had better go and find them from places less likely to be attacked. Eventually, thirty-four guns were found, ten from the west side of London and twenty-four from the provinces.

These new measures had immediate effect. On 12 August a flight of nine Gothas found a squadron of fighters rising in its path, turned about, jettisoned bombs and fled. On 22 August another force of Gothas crossed the coast at Margate and met with such a hot reception that they abandoned their plans and set about getting rid of their bombs on any target which presented itself on the way home. Two were shot down by aircraft from Manston, another fell to the Thanet Gun Defences, and a constant stream of gunfire pursued them along the coast to Dover, where more fighters appeared and chased them back to Belgium.

This reception so daunted the German commander that he reported that: 'the increased strength and better organization of the defences has now made it inadvisable to attack unless with machines which can fly loaded at over 3,000 metres or under cover of darkness'. This marked the virtual end of daylight raiding.

The first indication of a new German technique was revealed on 3 September with an attack that was spotted at 10.35pm off the North Foreland. Shortly afterwards, three or four Gothas appeared over Chatham; due to some unexplained delay in passing the warning, no alarm had been sounded and two 50kg bombs landed on the Drill Hall of the Naval Barracks, killing 130 naval ratings and wounding another eighty-eight. Several guns opened fire and sixteen fighters were sent up, but they saw nothing of the enemy. Among these fighters was Major Murlis-Green of 44 Squadron accompanied by Captain Brand and Lieutenant Banks, all flying Sopwith Camels. This was the first time that fighters of this type were flown at night and, much against general expectation, they landed the machines safely, thus clearing the way for future development of high-performance machines at night.

On the following night a force of ten Gothas attacked London, while another sixteen bombed a variety of targets in south-east England including Dover and Margate. Eight hundred shells were fired by the defences and one aircraft was brought down by a gun at Chatham. Eighteen fighter aircraft, including four Camels, went up but none made contact with the enemy.

A new defensive system was now set up: a line of balloons across eastern London, connected by cables from which wires were suspended so as to form a long 'apron' of cables into which an incautious raider might fly or over which a cautious one would have to climb. While this system was being implemented, a new scheme of barrage gunfire was worked out. The London sky was divided into squares, and patterns of barrage were calculated for each square to produce a curtain of shell bursts 2,500 feet (750m) deep at various heights. These areas were declared 'out of bounds' to aircraft and any aircraft seen or heard in them was assumed to be hostile and could be shot at instantly and without question.

Colonel Thompson of the Thanet Gun Defences devised an improvement to this, a system of height observation and control which, when he put it into operation, proved so effective that his guns shot down two Gothas. Strange to say (or perhaps not) he was immediately rebuked by the War Office for using an unauthorized method, but General Ashmore stepped in and took responsibility. The War Office then retaliated by forbidding the use of barrage fire at all and hamstrung some of Ashmore's gun sites by refusing to provide them with telephones. At this point Lord French intervened and gave General Ashmore a free hand. Colonel Thompson's system was standardized and, indeed, was to remain the standard system until it was replaced by radar in the latter part of World War Two.

Early in December 1917 a new threat appeared; the German Air Force had now begun to use the Giant Gotha, an enormous four-engined biplane. These could carry a bomb-load of 2,000kg (4,500lb) and they were well-provided with protective machine guns. Whether this latter feature led to feelings of self-confidence is not known, but certainly the first 'Giant' to attack England did so as an individual, crossing the coast near Ramsgate on the night of 5/6 December and dropping a few ineffectual bombs before returning home. Some hours after this a force of fifteen Gothas approached the coast and then split up, some going the usual route up the Thames Estuary to bomb Sheerness, while six swung in a loop across Kent and managed to get to London whilst the defences were concentrating on the river route. One unusual feature of this raid was that it was much later than usual; the raiders did not cross the coast until 2.00am, by which time most of the defence forces had decided that there was nothing likely to happen and had settled down for a quiet night. Another unusual point was that the bomb loads were mostly incendiary bombs; as a result the loss of life was minimal but the damage to property considerable.

The defences did very well; the barrage fire had discouraged the Sheerness raiders from coming further up the river and two Gothas were damaged sufficiently for them to have to make forced landings. One landed near Canterbury and was burned by its crew; the other landed near Rochford and was inadvertently burned by an RFC airman who, placed on guard, succumbed to curiosity and pressed the trigger of the German flare pistol 'to see if it was loaded'. It was. A third Gotha was seen to fall into the sea after clearing the coast and was assumed to have been damaged by gunfire.

General Ashmore now reasoned that the tools of the defence, the actual guns and aircraft, were as good as they were ever likely to be; the flaw lay in their application. In spite of arrows on the ground by day and searchlight indicators by night, the fact remained that once the fighter got off the ground it was no longer under anyone's effective control, and any interception made was more by luck than good management. What was needed was wireless communication with the pilot and, by the beginning of 1918, experiments in progress showed that this was no longer a pipe-dream but something that could be made to work. If it could, the next problem was what to tell the pilots, because the biggest flaw in the whole system was the method of reporting the movements of raiders. The distribution of observers was uneven and so was their performance. By collating reports gathered from observers it was possible, two or three days after a raid, to produce an elegant and accurate plot of exactly where the aircraft had been at any moment, but the information was no use by that time; it was wanted while the raid was on and the telephone reporting system then in use could not produce that sort of result. General Ashmore now set out on a massive reorganization of his observer and reporting system, a task which, in many ways, was a preview of his work six years later in setting up the Observer Corps.

Other moves made at the end of 1917 were the hastening of the balloon aprons around the eastern outskirts of London, setting them at 8,000ft (2,500m) height to force the bombers up and thus keep them in a relatively restricted belt of altitude, which made less sky for the fighters to search. Patrol lines were set up for the fighters, crossing the most likely enemy approach lanes and patrolling at 8, 9, 10 and 11,000ft, and the area beneath these patrol lines was emptied of guns but packed with searchlights.

As 1918 began, the London Defences mustered 249 guns, 323 searchlights, 89 day-fighters, 63 night-fighters and a number of wireless-equipped 'trackers'. On 28 January raiding began again when three Gothas flew up the Thames and spread out on both sides of the river to confuse the listening posts. One was shot

down as it was returning to the coast after dropping its bombs. Shortly after this a single Giant flew in, heading for London. It was caught over Essex by a Bristol Fighter, one of the newer machines used by the defence squadrons, but the Giant carried five machine guns and was a steady gun platform, and the fighter was beaten off, sustaining a punctured fuel tank and a wounded observer. After this the Giant continued in to Central London and dropped a number of bombs, one of which landed on a public air-raid shelter in Long Acre killing thirty-seven and wounding another eighty-nine people. It then turned about, evaded two lots of barrage fire, escaped another fighter, sliced through a balloon cable, and went home.

Although the defence forces were not to know it, the German bombing force at this time was at its lowest ebb: the Gotha Squadron, Kampfgeschwader 3, had suffered losses and the surviving members were worn out. It was decided to rest the squadron for several weeks and bring it up to full strength again.

Meanwhile the Giant Gothas, which formed an independent squadron, were to continue to raid as opportunity offered and, in fact, these half-dozen Giants were the only raiding force employed during the early months of 1918. Nevertheless, they kept the defences fully stretched, for, certainly at first, they appeared to be invincible.

By the late summer Ashmore had his reporting system thoroughly overhauled and ready to function. The delay had been due to difficulties in installing the multitude of telephone lines and in the need to try to build up the new system while keeping the old one working, so that there was no period in which the defences were devoid of some sort of communication. Every military unit under LADA command – gun site, searchlight, balloon apron, aerodrome – became an observing station, as well as police forces, coastguards and, where nothing else was available, specially installed posts were manned with either police or medically downgraded sol-

The Gothas had things their own way at first: the remains of Odhams Printing Works in Long Acre, London, after the Gotha raid on 28 January 1918.

diers. All these myriad of eyes were connected by telephone to one of twenty-five 'sub-control points'. Each sub control featured a large-scale map laid on a table, around which were a number of 'plotters' who were in direct communication with a group of observers. As the observers reported sight or sound of aircraft, so the plotters would place markers on the map to correspond, moving them to keep pace with the constant flow of information. One important feature of this system was that every telephone line was permanently connected; it did not pass through any telephone exchange, so there was no possibility of being disconnected and there was no waiting for connections.

Above the map table sat 'tellers' who were, in their turn, in direct communication by telephone with the LADA control room. This duplicated the sub control but on a larger scale, with a map table that encompassed the whole of the LADA area. The plotters at this table were being fed with information from the tellers of two or three sub-control rooms and they also placed markers on the map to indicate the progress of the raiders. An ingenious detail was the provision of a large clock, its face divided into coloured segments: as the minute hand entered a segment, the markers placed on the table were of that particular colour, so that watchers could immediately distinguish new information from old.

In a gallery overlooking the table sat Major-General Ashmore, accompanied by officers controlling the gun defences and the fighter aircraft, as well as representatives of the police and fire services. From the picture built up on the map, instructions were sent to fighter airfields and guns, to the balloon aprons and to police stations for warning purposes. From the fighter commander in the gallery a direct line ran to a powerful wireless transmitter near Biggin Hill from which orders were relayed directly to flight commanders in the air, for by the end of May the long-awaited wireless link had been perfected and was installed in selected aircraft. This arrangement was satisfactory for day work, since it would get the flight within visual pick-up distance of a raid; at night, a further refinement was the provision of short-range transmitters on the flight commander's machine and receivers in every fighter, so that the commands emanating from LADA control would be relayed to every machine in the air in a matter of minutes. Frequent exercises of the whole system soon tuned it to a perfect pitch, but, unfortunately, the whole splendid machine never went into action in earnest. The last German bomber had flown over England on 19 May 1918, four months before the LADA system got into operation.

THE USA

The first American move towards air defence came in 1915 when the Ordnance Department set about developing an anti-aircraft gun. Their first step was the obvious one of looking into the store cupboard to see what they had on the shelf that might be adapted to the task in hand. It would seem that the officers responsible for

the design were rather more forward looking than most and they seem to have had a more optimistic view of the development of aircraft than some of their European contemporaries, since with little hesitation they went for the most powerful gun they could find. Their choice fell on the 3-inch Seacoast Gun M1903, a 55-calibre gun firing a 15lb (6.8kg) high-explosive piercing shell at 853m/sec (2,800ft/sec) and with a maximum horizontal range of 10,355m (6.4 miles). Since it was thought that the principal role of an air-defence gun would be the protection of naval bases and dockyards, it seemed logical that the air-defence role should become the responsibility of the coast artillery branch, and thus selecting an existing coast gun would simplify matters. It would need some modification of the pedestal mounting to get more elevation, but little more needed to be done. There was a useful impact-fuzed high-explosive shell available and the existing 3-inch field-gun shrapnel shell could be taken into use and fitted into the coast gun's cartridge case if necessary. And so the 3-inch AA Gun M1917 came into being. A total of 160 were ordered to be built by Watertown Arsenal and the Bethlehem Steel Company, though it was well into 1920 before the order was completed and all the guns installed in various forts.

The first orders for the M1917 mountings (for there were plenty of guns on hand) was given in May 1916, and before that year was out the question of a mobile air-defence gun arose, a necessary protection for troops in the field. A design was drawn up using the ordnance of the 3-inch M1916 field gun; there was some sense in this because that gun was being developed on a split-trail carriage with ample elevation so that it could function as a field gun, but with the additional possibility of using it as an anti-aircraft gun when the need arose.

Unfortunately the 3-inch M1916 field gun was an early example of the designer biting off more than the production engineer could chew and, to cut a long story short, in 1917 the design

The American 'Mount, Improvized, M1917' was along the same lines as the German and French emergency designs. It was even supposed to be transportable.

was altered so as to allow the French 75mm Mle 1897 gun to be installed on the AA mounting. Fortunately, this didn't mean very much alteration, because the 'Mounting, Improvised, M1917' was a similar Heath Robinson design to that already developed by the French. It was mobile insofar as it could be dismantled, thrown on the back of a truck, taken somewhere else and then re-assembled, but that was the limit of its mobility. It was simply a structural steel frame that held the gun barrel and cradle at an elevated angle and allowed all-round traverse about a pivot sunk into the ground.

However, the Americans freely admitted that this was simply an emergency solution, of which only a handful were ever built, and, even before they entered the war, designs of a more respectable truck-mounted 3-inch M1916 gun

were in preparation. Again, this had to be changed to take the French Mle 1897 gun, and fifty were ordered without even waiting to see a pilot model. These eventually appeared mounted on White 30cwt trucks.

All these were hurried adaptations, simply because the American Expeditionary Force that sailed for France had to have some anti-aircraft guns. In the event, of course, they were provided with the French towed and automobile-mounted 75mm guns, and the few American-built guns and mountings that reached France appear to have been used for the protection of rear areas.

Meanwhile, the Ordnance Department designers had rolled up their sleeves and set about designing a completely new trailer-mounted AA gun. The first step was very simple; take the static mounted 3-inch M1917 and put it on a trailer. Unfortunately this was too simple a solution; in picking the M1903 Seacoast gun they had picked a very powerful weapon, one that was very satisfactory when on a permanent mounting emplaced in concrete. It was less of a success when fitted on to a trailer because it was far too powerful. Reinforcing or rebuilding the trailer to support the enormous recoil forces would have produced a cumbersome equipment and the designers, regretfully, had to abandon their idea and think again.

The 3-inch Seacoast Gun M1903 had been developed as a replacement for the 3-inch Seacoast Gun M1898; it was five calibres longer and used a larger cartridge case so as to generate more power. And, of course, armies are frugal organizations in that they rarely throw guns away until there is absolutely no possibility that they might be used again. So that after the Coast Artillery had replaced all its M1898 guns with M1903 guns, there was a large pile of elderly guns laid away in store. The next step in air defence was therefore fairly predictable; if the 1903 gun was too powerful, let's try the old ones. They did, and it worked. The M1898 Seacoast gun, suitably mounted on four-wheeled trailers

Battery B, 1st AA Battalion, 2nd Division, American Expeditionary Force, in action at Montreuil with their 75mm Autocanon, 5 June 1918.

The American 3-inch M1918 gun was trailer mounted and was an entirely different weapon from the static M1917, which had proved too powerful for the mobile role.

American soldiers explain the workings of their sound detector to a group of French schoolchildren. Ah, the wonders of modern science!

with stabilizing outriggers, became the 3-inch AA Gun M1918.

Which was all very fine, except that it burdened the anti-aircraft artillery with two totally different 3-inch rounds for the next twenty-odd years. The cartridge case for the M1918 mobile gun was 23 inches (58.4cm) long and of 212 cubic inches (3,477cc) capacity; that for the M1917 fixed gun was 26.7 inches (67.8cm) long with a capacity of 293 cubic inches (4,805cc). In practice, though, this was less of a problem than might be expected, because the two types of gun were rarely encountered in the same unit so that the ammunition types were usually well separated.

3 'The Bomber Will Always Get Through'

(Rt. Hon. Stanley Baldwin MP, 10 November 1932)

BRITAIN

As early as 1920, the Royal Artillery Committee, a subsidiary of the Ordnance Board that dealt with questions relating to artillery equipment, was looking to the new generation of anti-aircraft guns. In October 1920 they were asking whether it would be possible to put a 4.7-inch high-angle gun on to a tank chassis 'to give the required mobility'. They were informed that since the 4.7 with mounting weighed about 13 tons, a larger tank would be required, and 'it seems doubtful if it would appear a sound proposition to attempt the problem'. In the following month the Director of Artillery sent a memorandum to the Directors of Military Operations and Staff Duties, laying down what the regiment felt was desirable in new AA equipment:

A self-propelled caterpillar gun-mounting capable of all-round fire from 0 degrees to 90 degrees angle of elevation, with a maximum speed of 8mph and an economical speed of 3 to 4mph has been proposed. It is suggested that it should be able to negotiate slopes of 1-in-5 without becoming unstable. A very low emergency gear would be fitted to enable it to move in difficult places. One hundred rounds of ammunition would be carried in limber boxes on the mounting. It is thought advisable to consider the design with a view to transporting the complete equipment by rail. Is this desirable?

I should be glad to know whether you concur with the foregoing general particulars as they stand.

A month later, with Christmas safely over, the D of A was informed that DMO and DSD 'agreed with the general particulars'. Heartened by this he now set down more precisely what he had in view:

It would appear that the time has come for the method of traction for AA guns to be fully considered with a view to reaching definite decisions now that the work on the experimental guns and mountings is nearing completion.

It has already been decided that the 'primary' armament is to consist of 4.7-inch guns, and the 'secondary' armament of 3.3-inch or 3-inch guns (the comparative trials take place shortly at Shoeburyness).

No lorry is strong enough to carry even the lightest of these equipments, even if the rubber tyres permitted anything but usage on roads. The following suggestions are put forward:

For the 4.7-inch gun, in forward areas it should be mounted on a caterpillar tank; in rear areas and the Lines of Communication, it should be trailer-mounted; and in Home Defence locations it should be bolted down into prepared concrete emplacements.

The smaller gun should be similarly mounted, except that it would not be used in Home Defence.

Do you concur? The question is urgent if

provision is to be made for experiments in the Estimates for 1921–23.

A certain amount of debate followed this, and eventually it was decided that a self-propelled 4.7-inch was out of the question and that a suitable wheeled trailer should be designed. The problem was passed to the Superintendent of Design, and in June he produced a design that was 9ft (2.7m) wide, 12ft (3.6m) high and weighed 27 tons. The RA Committee: 'consider that, with an axle load of 13.5 tons and small wheels, such an equipment would not be able to move anywhere except on first-class roads. The Committee wish to be informed whether they are to proceed further with this question?' The Committee appear to have been told to forget it, since there is no further appearance of the trailer-mounted 4.7-inch gun in their minutes.

In March 1923, the D of A wrote to the Secretary of the RA Committee: 'This subject [i.e. AA equipment] is now re-opened. Please forward a definite recommendation as to which guns (3.3-inch or 3.6-inch) should be developed as the forward gun in mobile warfare, in place of the 3-inch 20cwt.' He also forwarded a decision taken by the Joint Air Ministry and War Office AA Technical Committee, which laid down the following as the ideal air defence gun:

- The heaviest shell consistent with efficient hand-loading
- Rate of fire at least twenty rounds per minute
- A minimum height range of 20,000ft at 4,000 yards
- Shortest possible time of flight to 9000 yards
- Mobility equal to that of the troops.

The Committee recommended that the 3.3-inch gun on SP tracked carriage should be developed.

In 1925 the question of self-propelled artillery arose and enough money was scraped together to develop an equipment which consisted of a Vickers medium tank-chassis carrying an 18-pounder (3.3-inch) field gun with a rather longer than usual barrel. This period, being one of economy, also saw a surge of ideas for dual- or even triple-purpose weapons; and the suggestion arose that if you had a 3.3-inch gun on a self-propelled mounting, you were rather more than halfway to reaching what the RA Committee had asked for two years previously. The design was altered to permit the gun to elevate to 85 degrees and traverse through 360 degrees. By November 1926 four guns were under construction and the Director of Artillery suggested that Vickers should be approached to develop a suitable sighting system for the air defence role.

These guns were eventually built and trundled around Salisbury Plain for a year or two with the experimental mechanized formations then being tried out. It was effective in its primary field role, less so in its secondary AA role, and if it did nothing else, it appears to have cured the itch for a dual-purpose field/AA gun faster than was achieved in other countries. The self-propulsion idea also got short shrift; the reasons for the abandonment of the experimental SP guns is not entirely clear, but there seems to have been an element of disagreement between the Royal Artillery and the Royal Tank Regiment as to who might be the proper organization to operate a self-propelled gun.

All of this had done nothing to help decide what the next generation of AA guns would be, so the Director of Artillery decided to start the ball rolling once more. In October 1928 he sent a memorandum to the Secretary of the RA Committee:

Assuming a war in which all existing stocks of 3-inch 20cwt HA guns are used up, is it recommended that replacement should be carried out (a) by the same type of gun, or (b) by a new design? In view of the low 'shell power' and ceiling of the present 3-inch equipment, would

The 3.6-inch gun had been developed in 1918–19 and was the principal hope for the future. Whilst a good design in many ways, it still had all the fire control on the gun, and loading it at high angles was a task for contortionists.

it not be advisable to go into the design of a gun firing a heavier shell?

The question now raised should be treated as entirely separate from the 4.7-inch AA equipment now under manufacture, as this equipment is only suitable for fixed or semi-permanent defences. Any new design must be suitable for the equipment of *mobile AA Units* and should, preferably, be capable of being mounted on the new Platform, Travelling, AA Mounting, No 2 Mark 1 recently introduced into the service.

Lastly, any such equipment would be most valuable if designed on the 'loose liner' principle, to enable rapid changing of liners in the field, as this would make the question of wear of secondary importance.

The RA Committee debated this and replied:

The Committee are of the opinion that in the present 3-inch 20cwt AA equipment the limit has been reached as regards shell power and ceiling combined with the mobility required by AA units in the field.

If, however, a less mobile but more powerful

Another view of the 3.6-inch gun, showing the difficulty of loading even at moderate angles of elevation.

The 3.6-inch gun on the move, though not, one suspects, at a very high speed.

A valiant attempt at a dual-purpose gun was the 18-pounder Mark 6. Mounted on a Vickers tank chassis, it was capable of acting as a field, anti-tank or anti-aircraft gun.

equipment is required for such purposes as the protection of vulnerable points on Lines of Communication, or for the inner defences of London, the Committee consider that a 3.7-inch gun firing a 25lb shell with a ceiling of, say, 28,000 feet would be effective and fill the gap between the medium (4.7-inch 50lb) and the light (3-inch 16lb) weapons.

That seemed a reasonable response, but before very much could be done about it the Depression struck and military finance dried up overnight. In spite of this, though, experimental work carried on at the Proof and Experimental Establishment, Shoeburyness, with various guns and types of ammunition, until a fairly tight specification had been hammered out. What was wanted was a weapon which would fire a 28lb (13kg) shell to 30,000ft (9,000m) at 3,000ft/sec (900m/sec), weighing less than 8 tonnes, capable of being brought into action in less than fifteen minutes and capable of being towed on hard roads at 25mph (40km/h). And when the ballistic calculations had been done it all pointed to a 3.7-inch gun.

By this time it was 1932 and the situation in Europe – and elsewhere – was beginning to look forbidding. Money was found and the specification was passed to Vickers Ltd with a request for a proposal that would meet it. In October 1934 they submitted a design and produced a wooden mock-up to show what the weapon would look like. After inspection and discussion, a few modifications and additions were requested, Vickers complied, and the first 3.7-inch Mark 1 guns went into service in January 1938. And make no mistake, at the time of its introduction the 3.7-inch was the most advanced gun of its type in the world and it maintained that lead for a very long time. Although remote power control, automatic fuze setting, mechanical loading and one or two other refinements were still a long way in the future, the mounting had been designed with these features in mind, so that when such things did arrive they could be fitted relatively easily and not demand a complete re-design of the equipment.

In July 1934 the design of the 4.7-inch gun, which had been the subject of experiment and development since 1919, was finally settled. It would fire a 50lb (23kg) shell at rather less than 2,500 feet a second (760m/sec) to 45,000ft (13,500m) and would be installed on semi-permanent emplacements for the protection of vulnerable points and rear areas, dockyards, naval bases and similar installations. But while Vickers and Woolwich Arsenal were preparing their proposals, the question of finance arose; a great deal of money had gone into the development of the 3.7-inch gun on high priority, and now these gunners were back again, cap in hand, asking for a very expensive 4.7-inch gun as well.

This impasse was overcome when somebody drew attention to the fact that the Royal Navy had a very good 4.5-inch high-angle gun that had a ballistic performance very close to the desired figures: a 54lb (24kg) shell, 2,400ft/sec (730m/sec) and a ceiling of 44,000ft (13,400m).

One of the first 3.7-inch Mark 1 AA guns to leave the factory, the most technically advanced gun of its day. The outriggers have not yet been fitted.

Another view of the 3.7-inch gun, complete with outriggers. Note the rope-and-pulley apparatus for hoisting the wheels off the ground so as to add to the mass and thus improve the stability.

A museum exhibit, this 3.7-inch Mark 1 is short of a few components but demonstrates how it went into action.

Moreover, it was designed and in production, and would therefore be a good deal less expensive than designing a new weapon from scratch. And since the army's future gun was intended to be used largely around naval installations or in home defence, it could be provided with naval ammunition without causing too much trouble in the logistic system.

The logic was irrefutable and the 4.7-inch design was dropped in favour of adopting the naval 4.5-inch gun. After some slight modifications to suit it to army practice and ancillary equipment, the 4.5-inch Gun Mark 2 entered army service in the summer of 1938.

The high-level threat was therefore taken care of; the low level threat had now to be addressed. By this time the threat was very real; air forces were developing multi-gun and cannon-carrying aircraft, as well as dive bombers, which were being used to assist their ground troops as a form of flying artillery, and something light and fast-firing, with a relatively short range, was what was wanted to counter these machines. But it was subject to the usual question – money. What was there in the cupboard that could be bodged or butchered to make a light anti-aircraft gun?

The only answer was the Vickers 2-pounder

The 4.5-inch gun on its 'Platform, Transporting'. The site was prepared with bolts set in concrete and the Platform carefully positioned above them; the platform was then lowered, nuts tightened down on the bolts, the wheels removed and the gun was ready for action.

The other side of the 4.5-inch gun; note the enormous counterweight, which balanced the preponderance of the barrel, a far cheaper but heavier option than a spring system used with the mobile 3.7-inch guns.

'Pom-Pom' used by the Royal Navy. This fired a useful shell at a rate of 60 rounds per minute and had an effective ceiling of 6,000ft (1,800m). The only trouble was that it was only available in a naval twin-mounting which weighed a fraction under 8 tons and was not mobile. However, time was getting short and in April 1937 it was decided to adopt the naval twin-mount for the defence of dockyards and naval bases, and then instigate a development programme to produce a new design of twin mounting capable of being moved more easily.

At the same meeting that arrived at this decision, agreement was also reached to adopt the Swedish Bofors 40mm automatic gun as the light air-defence weapon for use with the field armies.

The Bofors Company of Sweden had been in the gun-making business for centuries, building field and coast artillery weapons and having a successful export trade. In the 1920s they looked at what was available in the anti-aircraft field – which wasn't much – considered what was wanted, then set about designing. They produced two weapons; one was a 20mm cannon that had some degree of success in Scandinavia. The other was a 40mm weapon that was destined to arm three-quarters of the world.

The 40mm Bofors appeared in 1929 and made very little stir at first. It was automatic, with a sliding breechblock, fed by clips of four rounds that were dropped into feed guides above the breech, and it fired a 2lb shell at a rate of 120 rounds per minute. It was carried on a light four-wheeled trailer that could be brought into action very quickly by removing the wheels and spreading the outrigger legs to give a stable platform, or, in emergency, it could be fired off its wheels. Sales began in the early 1930s with the Baltic States and Scandinavia, after which Poland purchased a licence and began manufacturing their own guns. The British began to take an interest in the design in about 1933, attended various demonstrations, ran some tests and contemplated the matter, and eventually, in 1937 when some money appeared, placed an order with Bofors for 100 guns and a supply of ammunition. Very soon after that they went back for more, but by this time the word had spread and Bofors were working hard to fill all the orders that were flowing in and Britain found itself at the back of the queue. With Bofors' agreement, therefore, they went to the Poles who had now completed manufacture of the guns they wanted and were very happy to continue production and sell the result to Britain. These two orders filled the immediate needs, and now Britain negotiated a licence and began manufacture of guns, carriages and ammunition.

The 2-pounder Mark 8 twin gun, proposed as a static defence for dockyards and vulnerable points. A few were adopted but they were soon rendered obsolete by the Bofors gun.

The original Bofors 40mm, it almost looks flimsy by modern standards, but the simplicity of construction meant rapid production and low weight.

In the driver's seat: the simplicity of the Bofors is apparent in this view. The 'autoloader' is covered, to keep the rain out; the curved trough behind the gun deflects the ejected cartridge case and directs it forward, under the gun and clear of the mounting. The sight deflection was set by using the crossbar above the sights and the gunners looked through the two 'cartwheel' sights at their target.

FRANCE

The French, of course, would have nothing to do with the Bofors, adhering to their age-old policy of 'Support Local Industry', so they applied to their own gun makers for something similar. Hotchkiss had, as it happened, produced a small anti-tank gun of 25mm calibre that, for its day, was moderately efficient. They now looked at the Bofors and then back at their hand-operated Hotchkiss, and redesigned their gun into an automatic cannon, fed from a ten-round overhead magazine, which the French Army promptly adopted. By 1939 they had over 1,100 of these on two different mountings. Firing 350 285g (10oz) shells per minute, and

The French equivalent of the Bofors gun was the Hotchkiss 25mm automatic gun. Like the Bofors it used two gun layers and had a somewhat complex sighting system. The model aeroplane appears to have been some sort of on-carriage training simulator.

with a ceiling of 5,000m (16,500ft), it was probably as effective as the Bofors, making up in rate of fire what it lacked in shell weight.

Next, Hotchkiss (in the early 1930s) scaled-up the 25mm design to fire a 37mm round, seeking to improve the terminal effects. Schneider, the other major French private gun maker also essayed a 37mm design. Both firms produced guns, but it appears that Schneider concentrated on the export market, selling guns to Romania, Japan and some South American states, while Hotchkiss obtained contracts to supply the French Navy with twin-mounting guns for shipboard use. Although the army is said to have acquired some for their coast forts, evidence is lacking. These guns fired a 550g (19oz) shell, but their rate of fire was about the same as the Bofors and the ceiling was only slightly more than the 25mm gun, so it is perhaps understandable that there seemed to be little enthusiasm for them.

The 75mm Mle 1897 which featured so prominently in World War One was still in plentiful supply throughout the inter-war years, though by 1939 most of them had been refitted with longer barrels and provided with modern ammunition, so pushing the ceiling up to 8,200m (27,000ft). The shell was slightly lighter than the original pattern, but of higher-grade steel with more explosive filling and a streamlined shape which gave it better velocity and better 'carrying power' to maintain its velocity well up into the sky. The barrels were fitted to the old trailer mountings to become the '75mm Mle 17/34' and these formed the bulk of the French army's mobile air-defence force.

Two other 75mm guns appeared in the 1930s. The first looked exactly like the Mle 17/34 and was virtually the same weapon; the difference was that, whilst the 17/34 still adhered to the early idea of placing all the fire control on the gun sights, the Modele 1930 did away with the sights entirely and relied upon follow-the-pointer dials driven from a central predictor. The reasoning behind this appears to have been

The Schneider 90mm gun of 1926 looks deceptively spindly, but in fact weighed about 6 tons. For 1926 it was quite advanced, but barely a handful had been built by 1939, by which time it was obsolescent.

The Schneider DCA 90 gun in action. Note the unusual three-legged platform and the two large spring-casings linked to the barrel by wire ropes and pulleys so as to counteract the barrel weight.

that the Mle 17/34 could be used with field forces and could be dispersed in single guns or pairs or whatever combination the commander fancied, since every gun looked after its own arithmetic. The Model 30 would be used for what might be called 'semi-mobile' (or 'semi-permanent') defences, where a mobile force was available for deployment in a particular place for some length of time and could be connected to a predictor and an early warning system.

The second model used the same 53-calibre barrel as the Models 30 and 17/34 but placed it on an improved cruciform mounting. The original Mle 17 mounting was designed to be used with its rather large wheels in place, which gave the mounting a very high profile and a somewhat unsteady appearance. The new (1933) carriage used smaller wheels attached to a simpler carriage with the usual sort of pedestal, operating platform and four outrigger arms, and the wheels were removed when placing the mounting into action, so that the whole thing sat closer to the ground and was probably rather more stable. However, such was the slow pace of French re-armament in the 1930s that few of these guns were ever built.

So far Schneider had been constrained by the demand to use the existing gun and ammunition, but with the model of 1933 out of the way they were free to do some designing and come up with something of a more modern appearance. The result was the 75mm Mle 1936, with a slightly longer barrel and semi-automatic breech, on a carriage that was of the cruciform type but with rear trunnions so as to give a very low profile. It was, though, remarkable for its time in adhering to the practice of putting all the necessary fire control on to the carriage, so that it needed four gun layers to set and control everything while three men attended to the loading and firing. Again, although approved for issue, very few managed to get built before the outbreak of war.

The final shot in the French air-defence locker was the Schneider 90mm Modele 1926,

destined to be the heavy gun of the defences. It fired a 9.6kg (21lb) shell at 810m/sec (2,650ft/sec) to reach an 11,600m (38,000ft) ceiling and was mounted on a cruciform platform and pedestal. The most prominent feature was the balancing gear, to compensate for the weight of the barrel carried on rear trunnions. There were two very long spring casings at the front of the mounting, with cables running over pulleys to the gun cradle so that the springs took the weight of the barrel. Although quite a good design and with useful performance for its day, in the late 1930s it was decided to improve the mounting into the Mle 1939; this was simply a different method of arranging the wheels for transport and made no difference to the performance of the gun. But it was a waste of effort. Although this was the Modele 1926, only seventeen guns had been provided by September 1939, one of which had been appropriated as the prototype of the Mle 39 mounting.

THE USA

The Americans had used French 75mm guns for their anti-aircraft units in France in 1918, but this had simply been a matter of convenience; something to operate until their own designs started arriving in service. But like almost every other wartime American weapons project, by the time it started arriving in service the war was well over. By December 1918 only one complete 3-inch gun M1917 had been manufactured and delivered; the balance of the order for 160 was completed in 1919–20. A total of 612 M1918 mobile equipments had been ordered, but it is doubtful whether anything like that number was actually built, since most of the outstanding contracts were severely curtailed in 1919. This, though, proved to be sufficient for the needs of the peacetime army, and the various design offices were soon at work developing replacements.

Even before the war ended General Pershing,

This view of the Schneider 90mm gun shows the 1920s' thinking in the arrays of fire control equipment on the carriage.

commanding the American Expeditionary Force, had been making recommendations for new equipment, and he was particularly keen on air defence, demanding a heavy machine gun (which eventually appeared as the .50 Browning in later years) and a heavy 4.7-inch calibre anti-aircraft gun. On 11 December 1918, General Peyton C. March, Chief of Staff US Army, ordered the setting up of a board of officers to 'make a study of the armament, calibers and types of materiel, kinds and proportions of

ammunition and methods of transport of the artillery to be assigned to a field army'. They were to travel around Europe studying the artillery of Allied and ex-enemy armies, then return to the USA and visit military establishments and manufacturing plants as they saw fit. The board, consisting of three brigadier generals and four colonels, was headed by Brigadier General William I. Westervelt, from which it came to be called the 'Westervelt Board' or sometimes the 'Caliber Board', and its findings were to be the guidelines for the development of American artillery until the mid-1940s. What is worth remarking is that the board was convened in December 1918 and rendered its report to the Chief of Staff on the 23rd May 1919 – less than six months.

Since their remit was specifically restricted to field armies, the question of fixed defences was never approached. And in the fashion of the time, they began their observations by contemplating a dual-purpose field gun. In their discussion of field artillery they had specified an ideal maximum elevation of 80 degrees for divisional and corps artillery and of 65 degrees for heavier guns, and they now explained why:

> This is in view of the greatly increased air activity to be expected in the future and is with the expectation that the divisional and corps guns will often be used against airplanes, and the heavier types against balloons. These ideal types, however, are not yet practical and the following special anti-aircraft equipments are necessary. Moreover, special anti-aircraft weapons will probably always be required on account of the need for a higher initial velocity than is permissible in a general-purpose gun.
>
> Light Gun. Ideal. Caliber of about three inches with initial velocity of at least 2,600 ft/sec. Semi-automatic breechblock, mounted on carriage permitting 80 degrees elevation and 360 degrees traverse; projectile weighing not less than fifteen pounds, with one type high-explosive shell with maximum ballistic qualities and as large an explosive charge as possible; fixed ammunition, smokeless flashless powder, mechanical fuze. In this type every effort must be made to increase the rate of fire and decrease the time of flight; this latter is only limited by considerations of a reasonable accuracy life for the gun.

In fact, what the board was saying was 'smarten up the 3-inch M1918', since apart from the semi-automatic breech and mechanical fuze,

their recommendation was more or less descriptive of the existing equipment. They went on to recommend that it should be mounted on a tracked trailer and towed by a tracked tractor.

Next they considered the heavy gun, and it is obvious that they had been spoken to by General Pershing: '*Heavy Gun. Ideal.* a caliber of 4.7 to 5 inches, with initial velocity not less than 2,600ft/sec . . . projectile weighing forty-five pounds . . .', the remainder of the specification, relating to elevation, traverse, rate of fire and so forth, being word for word the same as for the 3-inch. That was the idea; the practical solution was 'arm units with the present 4.7-inch gun and continue experiments leading to development of the ideal', which is an interesting confirmation that as early as the spring of 1919 a 4.7-inch gun was actually in existence.

The Board also recommended that the 4.7-inch should be on a self-propelled tracked mounting, and in the following year this very thing appeared, developed by Walter J. Christie, who was shortly to become the guru of the tank world with his revolutionary high-speed vehicles. In 1920, though, he was content with a slow-moving platform that mounted a massive 4.7-inch gun. Not a lot is known about this particular gun, but it is remarkable in having a muzzle brake with, behind it, a large disc-type blast deflector. One is inclined to suspect that while the muzzle brake may have reduced the recoil, the gases leaving the brake and striking the deflector probably put back more energy into the recoiling parts than the brake had taken out.

This mounting appears to have convinced the designers of the 1920s that 'Black Jack' Pershing's 4.7-inch gun was a non-starter, too cumbersome to be practical. So if 4.7in was too big and 3in too small . . . let's try a 105mm and see how that looks. Development began late in 1924 and resulted in the Gun, 105mm M1927 on Mounting, AA Gun, M1926 – a very sophisticated piece of equipment. The gun was sixty calibres long, developing 854m/sec (2,802ft/sec)

General Pershing's 4.7-inch gun, on Christie's self-propelled mounting, being put through its paces in 1920. Neither of them got much further.

with a 14.5kg (32lb) shell and having a maximum ceiling of 12,800m (42,000ft). This was quite a startling performance for 1926 and, after some trials, it was standardized as the 105mm Gun M1 on Mount 105mm Gun M1 in 1927.

The mounting was a cranked pedestal that allowed an elevation of 80 degrees and all-round traverse, the whole thing being on a turntable that was sunk into a concrete emplacement. The gun had a semi-automatic breech and a compressed-air rammer mechanism, charged by a special cylinder forming part of the recoil system array, so that every time the gun fired it topped up the compressed-air reservoir. This allowed a steady twenty rounds per minute or a short burst, with pre-set fuzes, of thirty rounds per minute, though the normal rate with hand-set fuzes was restricted to fifteen rounds per minute. There was an electrical data transmission system that indicated the traverse

and elevation on dials for the gun layers to lay the gun by hand. Later in the 1920s the first experiments of remote power operation were carried out on one of these guns.

At the time of their approval, there was considerable debate about the method of gun construction to be adopted in the future. During World War One the 'auto-frettaged' system had been developed in France and Britain and was still in its infancy, but since it promised simpler and cheaper gun construction it was being followed up avidly by several countries. To understand what happened to the 105mm M1 we need to digress for a moment on the subject of gun construction.

Ever since Armstrong introduced his rifled breech-loading gun in the 1860s, gun construction had been a complicated business. The problem was how to obtain the necessary strength to withstand the explosion of the cartridge and the intense pressure inside the gun as

An early photograph of the first of the 105mm AA guns to be developed in the 1920s.

the shell was ejected – up to 20 tons per square inch was commonplace. Casting a piece of metal and then boring a hole in it meant that more metal had to be cast around the breech, where the pressure was greatest, and less around the muzzle, where the pressure was least. Armstrong showed how to do this by making a slender barrel and then shrinking additional 'hoops' or sleeves around it so as to build up the thickness and strength where it was needed. Heating the hoop to expand it, sliding it over the barrel and allowing it to cool squeezed the barrel and put the metal of the barrel into a state of compression, giving more resistance to the explosion.

Auto-frettage (or self-hooping) meant that the barrel could be made of one layer of steel that was then subjected to intense hydraulic pressure internally, a greater pressure than it would suffer from the explosion. This expanded the inner surface of the barrel beyond what is known as its elastic limit, so that it remained expanded. But the outer layers of the barrel metal did not expand beyond their limit and so, when the internal pressure was removed, they contracted back to their original state, so putting the inner layers of metal under a compressive pressure. The outer layers thus acted as a compressing hoop would have done on a plain steel barrel.

This technique was new and still being explored in the 1920s, and therefore there were some doubts about it. The 105mm M1927 gun was a one-piece ('monobloc') barrel, auto-frettaged. In case this was a failure, the M1 gun used a plain steel barrel bored out to a larger internal diameter and with an inserted auto-frettaged liner. And in case *that* was a failure

The 105mm M2 gun as installed in the Canal Zone. This is a somewhat confusing left-side view, not made easier by the accumulation of fuze setter and data transmission equipment that has been crowded on to the mounting.

there was also an M2 gun using a thicker liner that was not auto-frettaged and which had the main body of the gun shrunk around it. Exhaustive firing trials with all three guns were then carried out, at the end of which it was con-sidered that the loose-liner systems showed no particular technical advantage in this particular gun, and that as the original monobloc auto-frettaged gun was the cheapest of the three types, it would henceforth be standardized as the M3 gun. This was formalized in 1933, at which point the army was told there was no money in the till and they would have to wait for their guns.

In 1936 the money was found, and in 1937–38 fourteen guns were built and issued, the major-ity of them going to forts in the Panama Canal Zone. There they stayed until 1944 when they were replaced by 120mm guns, and the 105mm M3 was declared obsolete in February 1945, one of the few American artillery weapons to be made obsolete before the war ended. What went wrong? Ten years of development and testing, fourteen guns completed, never a shot in anger, and scrapped inside seven years?

It wasn't a question of what went wrong, it was a question of something going so right that it outperformed the 105s and made them obso-lete as soon as they had been emplaced. At the same time as the 105mm M3 gun finally went into production, the Coast Artillery Board (who were still responsible for air-defence artillery in 1938) decided that the 3-inch gun was now obsolete and that a replacement had to be found, and quickly. The Board were quite open minded about calibre, but insisted that the shell had to weigh at least 21lbs (9.5kg) – so as generate a decent lethal area in the sky – with the upper limit of weight to be governed simply by the need to load the gun manually. Powered rammers were all very well for permanently emplaced guns, but had no place on mobile guns for field use that had to be manhandled into position. So the complete round of ammu-nition had to be something that the average fit soldier could keep on lifting and loading for a reasonable period of time.

One supposes that the design offices had run various solutions past their drawing boards over the years, and the Coast Artillery Board were soon given a solution to their problem, a 90mm gun firing a 24lb (10.9kg) shell. While still arguing for a 21lb shell and more velocity, the Board approved the proposal and in June 1938 the development of the 90mm Gun T2 was authorized. Further proposals led to the authorization of the Mounting, 90mm, T1 in August 1938; work moved ahead smoothly and the two designs were approved and standardized as the 90mm Gun M1 on Mounting M1 in March 1940.

Meanwhile, experiments continued. The US 3-inch M1923E was just one of many weapons developed in the search for the ideal gun.

While all this had been going on, the 3-inch guns had been the sole operational anti-aircraft equipments, and there had been various shifts and improvements from time to time in order to keep them at least nominally serviceable. The principal change, so far as the guns went, was in the matter of construction. Both these guns, the M1917 static and the M1918 mobile, stemmed from turn-of-the-century ancestors that were built up from hoops and tubes in the traditional fashion. They were designed when guns fired a few rounds a year and lasted a long time before the rifling was worn to the point of inaccuracy. But an anti-aircraft gun was a different proposition; it could fire more rounds in a single engagement than most coast defence guns fired in a year. Consequently they wore out quickly, and dismantling a built-up gun to put in a new rifled bore was a long and difficult business. So the first thing was to redesign them with loose liners that could be changed in the field or in the emplacement without having to take the gun to an engineering works. The M1917 gun was therefore re-designed into a simple tube and loose liner, thus becoming the 3-inch gun M2. At the same time the twist of rifling was changed. In the original M1903 gun the rifling increased its rate of twist as the shell moved up in the bore, beginning at one turn in fifty calibres and gradually tightening to one turn in twenty-five at the muzzle. This was a popular scheme in the 1890s, since it reduced the initial torsional stress on the driving band as the shell began to accelerate. It was also claimed to reduce wear, but experience showed that this was questionable. Improved methods of seating the driving band allowed greater stress to be absorbed and, since uniform-twist rifling was easier to cut, a uniform twist of one turn in twenty-five calibres was adopted. However, at much the same time there was a lot of work being done on mechanical time fuzes for the anti-aircraft shells; these relied upon centrifugal force to provide the driving power, and the 1/25 twist of rifling proved to be too abrupt for the fuze mechanism to run reliably. It was therefore changed again, this time to one turn in forty calibres.

The M2 gun was quite satisfactory so far as ballistics went, but the manufacture was a little difficult, and so a third design appeared; the change was merely a matter of making the loose liner thicker, which allowed a relaxation of the tolerances between liner and barrel, but it simplified manufacture as well as speeding it up and reducing costs, and this now became the M4 gun in 1928. This was heavier than the original M1917, so the mounting was redesigned with heavier trunnion bearings and cradle, and became the Mounting M1.

The development of the mobile gun was even more involved, largely because it turned into a search for the perfect mounting.

The development of the gun followed the same process as that of the static equipment; indeed, it actually preceded it, since the army considered that the mobile gun was more important than the static one. Since the Westervelt Board had asked for the development of a 3-inch weapon, there was a good deal of incentive for the designers and several designs were contemplated in the early 1920s before the financial barriers appeared. Eventually, in 1927, the 3-inch Gun M1 was standardized, fifty calibres long and with the same sort of liner construction as the M2. As with the M2 it was seen that a heavier liner would simplify construction and this led to the adoption of the M3 in 1928. And note, too, that the numbering system made it easy to distinguish between the guns: odd numbers were mobile, even numbers static.

The mounting was a different matter. The original mobile mounting developed for the M1918 equipment, in the days when nobody knew very much about anti-aircraft equipments, was not a bad first attempt, but as time

The final design of static 3-inch gun, the Gun M4 on Mount M3, was a neat and workmanlike equipment. Note the fuze-setting machine below the breech (actually to the right of it) and the cables for delivering data to the gun layers' dials.

went on it was obvious that it could stand improvement. It was little more than a four-wheeled flatbed trailer with two stabilizing out-riggers and levelling jacks on each side. On top of this went the pedestal mount for the gun, with seats for the gun layers and a tiny platform for the breech operator and loader.

After a good deal of experimenting and re-thinking, the M1 mount appeared in 1927. It was still a rectangular four-wheeled trailer, but now had extremely long outrigger arms on each corner; these were hinged to the platform and had a second hinge in the centre of their length so that they folded up in the middle and then folded back to lie on the platform. This double fold soon gave rise to the nickname 'Spider Mount', which stuck to both it and its follow-ers. The gun was on the usual sort of pedestal mount in the centre of the platform and there were segments of perforated metal platform, which folded down and rotated with the gun to form a working surface for the gun detachment.

A handful of these M1 mounts were made and issued and given a thorough trial by the gunners, after which various improvements

were made. The weight was reduced by increased use of aluminium and welded steel components, and various minor operating problems were sorted out. These improved models became the M2, which then went into quantity production. In the mid-1930s the M2A1 appeared, with an improved jacking and levelling system and a new method of carrying the spare wheels on elevated mounts, Finally, in February 1938, came the Warner Electric Brake craze in which virtually everything in the US Army that was to be towed had electric internal-expanding brakes fitted, operated automati-cally by the towing vehicle. Which was fine, so long as the right towing vehicle was used. When fitted with these brakes, the mounting became the M2A2.

The last of the between-wars American guns to be considered is the lightweight 37mm gun, intended for close defence against ground-attack machines. There is a certain amount of confusion over this gun, because the Westervelt Board recommended a 37mm infantry gun and it has sometimes been assumed that the AA gun stemmed from this. The two were completely

The 3-inch Gun M3 on Mounting M2 was the field army mobile gun.

The 3-inch Gun M3 on Mounting M2 in the travelling position.

different; the Westervelt Board envisaged a light infantry-accompanying gun, similar to that which the French had developed in 1916 and issued to the AEF. By 1923 the Infantry Board had reached the conclusion that it was a useless device and more trouble than it was worth and had thrown the idea out, although it returned periodically until the 1940s and wasted a good deal of people's time. The AA gun was the result of an entirely different enterprise.

At the end of World War One there was a great deal of activity in all the combatant countries to develop large-calibre guns for use in aircraft. Several designs had been put forward in the USA and one, the Baldwin 37mm automatic gun, was being favourably considered. It was, in fact, an American version of a French copy of a British design, but we need not explore that

aspect. It failed to come up to expectations and, in late 1920, the Ordnance Department called in John M. Browning to have a look at it and perhaps suggest some solution to its shortcomings. The eventual solution was simply to throw the thing out and start all over again, and thus although the Baldwin was a failure it at least has the merit of having interested John Browning in a heavy calibre automatic weapon.

By April 1924 Browning had produced two prototypes and demonstrated them at Aberdeen Proving Ground. He then passed it to Colt's to undertake the further development, fine-tuning and production engineering aspects of the design work, This moved slowly, for there was little incentive in the early 1920s; John Browning died in 1926 and in the following year the gun as it then stood was given 'Limited

Pre-war drill with the mobile 3-inch gun on the 'Spider Mount'.

Procurement Type' status, after which all development stopped, and the design was shelved.

Browning had actually produced two different guns, one designed for a velocity of 400m/sec (1,300ft/sec) and the other for 610 m/sec (2,000ft/sec), since by that time the Ordnance Department had decided that, in addition to using the 37mm gun *in* aircraft, it might very well also be used *against* them, and possibly even as the infantry gun the Westervelt Board had postulated. The gun design bore no relationship to Browning's well-known machine gun; it was a long-recoil weapon using a vertical sliding breechblock and was fed from a ten-round clip. The aircraft gun was revived in 1929 and licensed to Armstrong-Whitworth in Britain before returning to the USA and being taken up again in the 1930s, but the anti-aircraft gun remained on the shelf until 1935,

when work began on developing a suitable carriage.

The gun was eventually approved as the M1 and fired a 21oz (600g) high-explosive shell at a rate of 120 rounds per minute. The muzzle velocity was 792m/sec (2,600ft/sec); it had an effective ceiling of 3,200m (10,500ft) and a maximum ground range of 8,115m (8,850 yards). Theoretically the gun could reach out to an altitude of 5,870m (19,300ft), but the shell was fitted with a self-destroying device that blew it up after 3,200m (10,500ft) of vertical travel or 3,650m (4,000 yards) of horizontal flight.

The first carriage was the M3, a four-wheeled trailer with the wheels carried on two detachable axles. The gun was mounted on a levelling block that could be adjusted to correct up to 10 degrees for the trailer being out of level. Unlike larger anti-aircraft mounts, this had no jacking system and therefore the trailer had to be brought into action on a piece of ground with less than 10 degrees of slope in any direction before the wheels were removed. The top carriage, the portion that was levelled, carried the gun, sights, seats for the layers (two – one for line and the other for elevation) and a platform for the loader. Operation for elevation and traverse was entirely manual and sighting was by open sights.

The Gun M1A2 on Carriage M3 was formally standardized in 1938. Manufacture began in 1939, with Watervliet Arsenal manufacturing the guns, Rock Island Arsenal the carriages, and Bausch & Lomb the sights. Gun manufacture was later extended to Colt's, but in February 1941 they were instructed to put the AA gun to one side and concentrate on aircraft cannon. By that time the 40mm Bofors gun was being discussed, but the Ordnance Department was reluctant to scrap all the research and

investment that had gone into the 37mm gun and they successfully argued for its continuance in production. It was as well that they did; 40mm gun production was never sufficient to replace the 37mm and it served throughout the war, some 7,728 complete equipments being built before production ended in 1944.

In 1937 the US Navy became interested in the Bofors gun as a possible shipboard air-defence gun. There appear, however, to have been some glorious misapprehensions and misunderstandings between the Navy and the Bofors Company, and at much the same time a Mr Hudson of the Washington Navy Yard appeared with a design for a 1.1-inch heavy machine gun that promised to be the answer to the Navy's problem. Interest in the Bofors dwindled, and it was to be neglected until 1940.

The Hudson machine gun, though not strictly artillery, is worth a mention because Hudson's basic idea was for a recoil-reducing

The US 37mm Gun M1 on Carriage M3A2: note the remote power-control motors and the receiver dials for operating with a predictor.

mechanism that, he claimed, could be applied to any weapon up to 3-inch calibre. In brief, his machine gun was a gas-operated weapon with a gas cylinder beneath the barrel; but instead of blowing a piston backwards to operate the mechanism, like most other gas-operated guns, the Hudson first blew a weight forward to arrive at the front end of the cylinder and hit a spring buffer just as the bullet was leaving the muzzle, so that the forward-flying weight compensated for the rearward movement due to the gun's recoil. The arrival of the weight then allowed a conventional gas-piston to operate the extraction and reloading cycle and, as the gun's bolt went forward, so the weight moved back into its rest position. All very complicated but it worked, and it did what Hudson claimed; reduced the recoil force and thus reduced the deck blow to the ship's structure. The US Navy was sufficiently impressed to build a large number of quadruple mountings carrying four 1.1-inch Hudson guns and fitted them to a number of warships.

GERMANY

One of the advantages of losing a war is that you also lose all your equipment, so you can start with a clean sheet instead of having to keep using your obsolete equipment for the next twenty years, like the victors. The Versailles Treaty stripped Germany of almost all its anti-aircraft guns; only a handful in the Fortress of Königsberg being permitted to the army and another handful on board the few warships left to the navy. All the myriad wartime expedients were swept away and melted down for scrap. The flame of air-defence knowledge was kept alight by various subterfuges; army artillery officers were attached to warships as 'liaison officers' but they spent most of their time liasing with the anti-aircraft gunnery officer. A number of wartime anti-aircraft guns were 'converted' into field guns by modifying the carriages,

removing the anti-aircraft sights and fitting elevation stops on to the elevating arc to prevent the gun barrel being raised above 35 degrees or so. They were then issued to field artillery units 'in lieu' of conventional field guns, one motorized battery of these converted weapons being attached to each of the seven artillery regiments permitted under the Treaty. The anti-aircraft sights and equipment were spirited away and hidden.

Germany had no illusions about the need for air-defence guns; it was surrounded by potential enemies and air attack might come from any direction, and it was not permitted an air force. Training, equipping and organizing an air force, when it was permitted, was going to take time, and would be complicated by the fact that aircraft design was advancing in leaps and bounds. By comparison, gun design was less affected by technological change, so plans for gun production could be drawn up with every chance that they would be able to go into production very rapidly and thus provide protection while the air force was being put together. And so gun designers beavered away, some in drawing offices in Germany well separated from their parent factories so as not to attract attention from the Disarmament Commission inspectors, some in neutral countries where companies had pre-war links with German firms which had not been severed by the war. Krupp, for example, sent a number of its designers off to work in the Bofors drawing office in Sweden, while Rheinmetall acquired a Swiss machine-tool company and sent their designs there to be prototype engineered.

Rheinmetall had, in fact, begun by opening a subsidiary office in Holland, selling war-surplus weapons on the export market, largely for the benefit of those small nations that had no armaments industry and limited finances. They also attempted to promote the wartime 20mm Erhardt aircraft cannon under a different name, but with little success, and they eventually sent the cannon off to their Swiss office, Solothurn

AG, with instructions to overhaul the design and turn it into a light anti-aircraft gun, for which there appeared to be a better market.

Although the German Army was denied anti-aircraft weapons by the Treaty, it achieved a head start in the light AA field by simply obtaining an agreement that anything less than 25mm was a machine gun; with this settled it was among the first armies to adopt the 20mm Oerlikon, as the '2cm Flak 28' gun. This was only adopted in small numbers but it was sufficient to give some experience and convince them of the utility of this sort of weapon.

In 1933 Adolf Hitler became Chancellor of Germany and within a few weeks the designers began returning home with the results of their work. The engineers from Solothurn produced their S5-100 20mm cannon, and the army began evaluating it as a possible light AA gun. More important, however, was the package of drawings brought back by the Krupp design team who had been lodging with Bofors; this contained drawings of an entirely new 88mm anti-aircraft gun, destined to become the most famous gun of World War Two and possibly of the entire century. The army took one look at the drawings and approved it forthwith without the formality of pilot models and trials. Krupp could be relied upon to produce a combat-worthy weapon without needing any urging. And Krupp began preparing tooling against the day when manufacture would no longer be restricted by Treaty obligations.

The 'Eighty-Eight', as it came to be known, was no wonder gun; at the time of its initial acceptance by the German army it was probably the best anti-aircraft gun in the world, but it did not hold that position for very long. The reason that the 88 became famous was simply because there were a lot of them, more than any comparable weapon, more than many better weapons, and the Germans, less worried by hierarchic precedent, were not averse to using it for any task which came along. It therefore appeared as an anti-aircraft gun, an anti-tank gun, a field gun, a coast-defence gun, a submarine gun, a tank gun…there seemed to be nothing this gun could not do.

The original model, which went into service in 1933, was known as the 'Flak 18'. This was a deliberate piece of deception applied to other military equipment at that time. There had been, as we know, an 88mm Flak gun in 1918; therefore calling the new gun the Flak 18 suggested to any casual observer that this was simply the 1918 gun with new tyres and a coat of paint. (The same piece of misdirection was used with the 105mm field howitzer, another weapon which had a 1918 ancestor.) But the new gun was a far more powerful weapon than its predecessor and with greatly improved ammunition. Moreover, it was provided with dials for receiving firing data directly from the predictor, as well as with indirect-fire sights for firing against ground targets.

In 1936 the German government sent the 'Condor Legion' to Spain to render some assistance to General Franco and, in doing so, give some hands-on experience to the troops and some practical testing to their new equipment. Since the air element formed a major component of the Legion, some 88mm Flak 18 guns were sent along to protect their airstrips. As a result of this experience, and of reports from training units in Germany, some modifications were made. The carriage changed from an octagonal platform with outriggers to a square platform with outriggers of the same pattern all round rather than different types for front and rear. The system of jacking and spreading the legs was simplified, as was the method of removing the two axles, and both axles now had twin wheels.

The most remarkable change lay in the construction of the gun. The original weapon was a single-tube barrel carried in a jacket attached to the cradle and recoil system. The new barrel was in three pieces – a chamber section, centre section and muzzle section – a design that conferred considerable advantages. Firstly, instead

The German 88mm Flak 18 on tow behind the standard prime mover, the 8-ton Zugkraftwagen. *This is a photograph of equipment captured by the British, hence the somewhat battered appearance of the front mudguard.*

The 88mm Flak 18 in travelling order. Note the shield, an original piece of equipment that was quite quickly abandoned, and the crank apparatus between the front wheels, used for lowering the platform and removing the wheels.

View - left front - travelling.

of having to change the whole barrel when the commencement of rifling wore away due to the high temperature and pressure inside the chamber, only the rear section, which carried the first few inches of rifling, needed to be changed. Secondly, the three sections could be made from different steels, so confining the more expensive and difficult material to the part that needed it; and thirdly, making the barrel in short lengths meant that contractors did not

have to have very long gun-lathes in order to make replacement barrels, thus easing production, since barrels are usually the bottleneck in gun production. The reverse side of the coin was, as might be imagined, the need for a very high standard of precision and minimum tolerances in manufacture. This improved model went into production early in 1937 as the Flak 36; visually there was practically no different between it and the Flak 18.

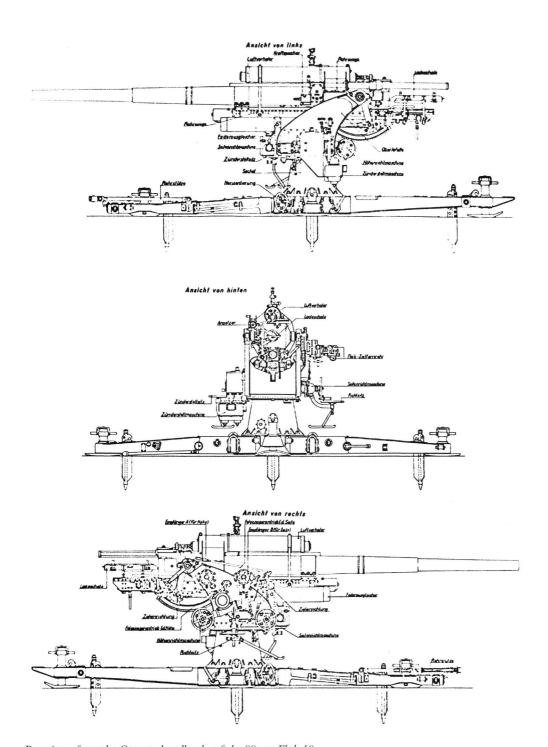

Drawings, from the German handbook, of the 88mm Flak 18.

Spain had also shown the gun's potential as an anti-tank gun, as a result of which an armour-piercing shell was provided and a telescope sight fitted for direct shooting. Finally, the fire-control system was improved and follow-the-pointer dials were installed in place of the original receiver dials. These held two pointers, one driven by the predictor and the other by the actual movement of the gun; all the gun layers had to do was watch their dial and, as the predictor pointer moved, so they operated their elevation or traverse control wheel and 'followed the pointer' to match its position. With all these improvements in place the gun now became the Flak 37.

The Flak 18/36 weighed just less than 5 tons, so it could be towed by a wide selection of vehicles and with a well-trained detachment could be brought into action very quickly, and even fired off its wheels in extreme emergency. So the army and Luftwaffe were satisfied that they had a sound medium-calibre mobile gun. (Although the Luftwaffe was responsible for Flak artillery in Germany, outside Germany and in the field it was the army's business, hence their interest in the 88mm gun.) However, the Luftwaffe were of the opinion that, the speed of development of aircraft being what it was in the 1930s, a heavier weapon with a higher reach, static mounted for the defence of cities in Germany, would be a

Follow-the-pointer dials on a German 88mm AA gun built by Krupp for sale to the Argentine in 1938. The predictor pointer is the white triangle on the outside of the dial figures; the gun pointer is the large finger on the inside of the dial.

The 88mm Flak 37 with improved barrel and data transmission system.

good investment, and late in 1933 (when, bear in mind, the Luftwaffe did not officially exist . . .) a demand was raised for a 10cm gun, provisionally entitled 'Gerät 38'.

The specification, which was given to both Krupp and Rheinmetall, demanded full-power operation, a high rate of fire, reasonable road mobility and, of course, the best ballistic performance possible. The two companies were each to produce two prototypes, one using hydraulic power and the other electrical power, after which they would be asked to produce four pre-production equipments for extended troop trials. The prototype stage saw a good deal of chopping and changing as various ideas were tried and rejected, but eventually the two trial batteries were put through their paces in the spring and summer of 1936. In October 1936, after careful analysis of the troop trials, the Rheinmetall gun with hydraulic power control was selected for production as the 10.5cm Flak 38. It fired a 14.5kg (32lb) shell at 880m/sec (2,900ft/sec) to a maximum height of 11,400m (37,500ft), which was very satisfactory, and the only complaint levelled at it was that it was rather cumbersome to move – weighing 13.5 tons (13.7 tonnes) behind the towing vehicle – and took some twenty minutes of hard work to get into action. But as the weapon had been specified as static equipment for home defence rather than mobile field equipment, these were not really valid complaints.

The 105mm Flak 38 was probably the first anti-aircraft gun in any army to have a fully mechanized loading system. The complete fixed round, shell and cartridge, weighed 26.5kg (58lb) and was 1.164m (3ft 10in) long, something of a handful to lift chest-high and throw into the breech. So there were two loading trays, an electrical fuze-setter, and roller ramming-gear set into the breech ring. The loader came along to the side of the gun carrying the round

A rarely-seen stage in the development of almost every gun is the full-scale wooden model, which gives the user an idea of what he is about to receive. This was the model of the 105mm Flak 38.

The finished article (in this case the actual 105mm Flak 38) is usually rather less sleek and elegant than the model was.

of ammunition and dropped it into the first loading tray; this rocked upwards, lifting the round into line with the fuze setter, which slid back over the fuzed shell and set the fuze according to data transmitted from the predictor. The setter moved away, the tray rocked again and dumped the round into the second loading tray, which then rocked across in line with the chamber of the gun. As it did so, the nose of the shell entered the jaws of the breech ring. Inset into the breech ring were two double-cone-shaped rubber rollers that were gently turning, driven by a hydraulic motor. As the forward section of the shell passed between these rollers, the tray tripped a valve that caused the two rollers to contract and grip the shell firmly. At the same time, the motor accelerated and the rollers speeded up, pulling the shell and cartridge off the loading tray and propelling them into the breech. As the cartridge-case rim left the tray it tripped a lever, which caused the tray to swing back, clear of the path of recoil, the breechblock was released and closed and the gun fired. The rollers then retracted into the breech ring during the recoil stroke, so that as the breechblock opened and the empty case was ejected, it had a clear exit path through the breech ring. And as the gun ran back into battery, so all the various components re-set themselves ready for the next round.

The hydraulic motors were driven by electric motors using direct current from a generator that formed part of the battery equipment. In 1939 the design was changed to use alternating current, so that the normal commercial and domestic supply could be tapped into in static sites, with AC generators provided for emergency use. The gun barrel, originally a single tube, was changed to a five-part tube along similar lines to the improved 88mm barrel, and the improved follow-the-pointer data transmission system was adopted, also similar to that adopted with the 88mm gun. With all these changes the equipment now became the 105mm Flak 39.

Like any other military force, the Luftwaffe was never satisfied with what it had, but was always lusting after something better, and in 1936, having seen the 105mm gun on its way to production, when they asked for something even bigger and better, they were given a free hand to draw up a specification and start development of a 12.8cm (5in) gun.

In fact, after carefully considering the likely future performance of bomber aircraft, their probable speed and altitude, it was decided to start two parallel lines of development, one for a 12.8cm gun, and one for a 15cm gun. As usual, both the major gun makers were given contracts, but the 12.8cm gun was contracted solely to Rheinmetall; the 15cm weapon was, at first, contracted solely to Krupp, but later a second 15cm contract went to Rheinmetall.

The prototype 12.8cm gun was submitted for test in the late summer of 1937 and was an immediate success, being ordered into production as the 12.8cm Flak 40. In general appearance it was simply an enlarged 10.5cm Flak 38; it used a similar sliding block breech, and a similar fuze-setting and roller ramming-system, driven by hydraulic motors. The mounting was provided with seats for the gun layers and platforms for the loaders and breech operator; these platforms were on pivoted arms that were controlled by the movement of the gun, so that no matter what the elevation, the gunners were always in the same position relative to the gun breech.

The price for all this was, of course, weight; the gun weighed just over 12 tons in the firing position and, because of this, it had to have the barrel removed before it could travel. The mounting, the usual sort of platform with four outriggers, was jacked up and a two-wheeled limber rolled underneath each end, but the barrel had to be disconnected from the recoil system and slid out of its cradle and into a special transport wagon. While this system had been written into the specification and approved when the gun underwent its acceptance trials, a

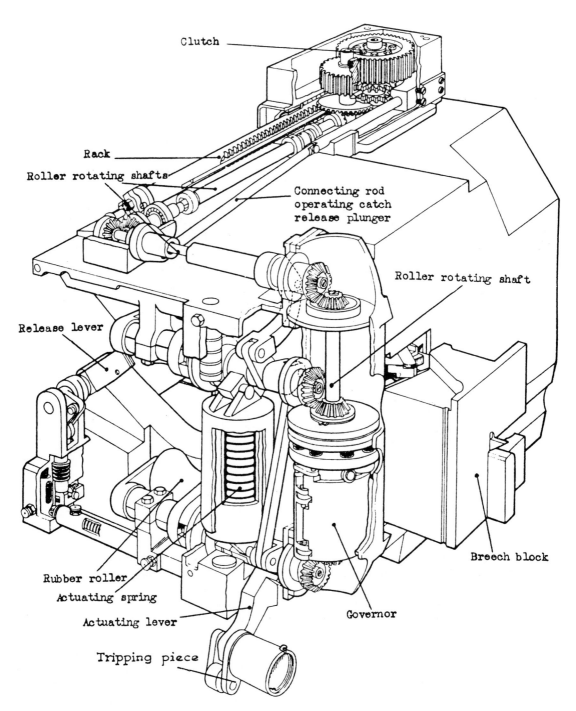

Clutch

Rack

Roller rotating shafts

Connecting rod
operating catch
release plunger

Roller rotating shaft

Release lever

Breech block

Rubber roller

Actuating spring

Actuating lever

Governor

Tripping piece

A diagram of the roller ramming gear for the 88mm Flak 41, which was practically the same as that used with the 105mm and 128mm guns, different mainly in scale.

The German 128mm Flak 41. Like most static guns the platform was relatively simple and relied upon being securely bolted down into concrete

short period of service experience soon showed that this was no way to move an anti-aircraft gun if you needed it in a hurry – which was frequently the case. So late in 1938 a number of vehicle specialists were approached by the Luftwaffe to see if they could provide a better solution.

The eventual answer was actually devised by the Army Weapons Office and built by the Meiller Company. It was apparent that there was no need for the outriggers on the platform; these were fitted to mobile AA guns simply to spread the load and resist recoil thrust no matter where the gun was pointed. But the 12.8 was to be bolted down by twelve heavy bolts to a holdfast set in concrete, so the outriggers were quite superfluous. The mounting thus became a simple rectangular girder structure carrying the usual gun pedestal; attached to the ends of this platform were two cantilever arms, the outer ends of which rested on four-wheeled limbers. These had independent suspension, together with hand pumps for lifting and lowering the gun platform by hydraulic means, and also

winches for manoeuvring in difficult terrain. The result was an elegant technical solution, but it was 15m (49ft) long and weighed about 26 tons (26.5 tonnes), which does not sound like the easiest thing in the world to tow around the countryside.

In the event few were ever made; by the time the design was perfected and the guns began to come off the production line in 1942, the manufacture of mobile guns above 105mm calibre had been prohibited, and all subsequent production was simply of the gun and its basic pedestal, ready for bolting down into concrete or, as subsequently happened, mounting on railway wagons.

At the other end of the scale, the field armies wanted some lightweight weapons which they could deploy against ground-attack aircraft without having to go through all the rigmarole of laying out guns, cabling them up to predictors, and so forth and so on. They wanted instant response and their existing Oerlikon Flak 28 was not sufficient for the job.

This is where Rheinmetall stepped in with

The quick solution to increasing firepower – double the guns. These twin 128mm guns were developed for mounting on Flak Towers in major German cities.

Another handbook illustration, this time of the German 2cm Flak 38 in the firing position and in the travelling mode. The Flak 38 was simply the Flak 30 modified to produce a higher rate of fire.

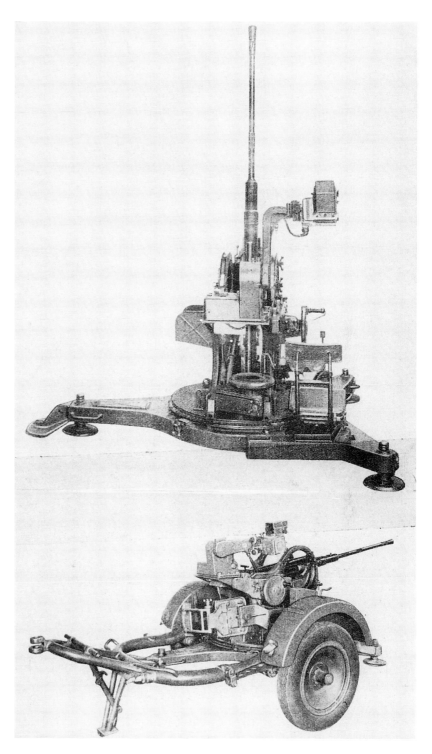

their Solothurn design, which was promptly adopted as the 2cm Flak 30 by the German navy in 1934 and by the army in 1935. The gun itself was nothing more than the Solothurn MG30 machine gun scaled up to take a 20mm cartridge – a recoil-operated machine gun firing from an open bolt and using a box magazine. The carriage was a highly mobile trailer, light enough to be towed by almost any vehicle, and on this was the gun mounting, secured by two lugs and a simple release pin. By pulling the pin and allowing the trailer to tip up, so as to let the mounting touch the ground, the retaining lugs came free and the trailer was simply slid away from beneath the gun mount. It could then be levelled by its three adjustable feet, the gunner climbed into his seat behind the breech, the loaders stood by with full magazines and the gun was ready for action. And if things were really desperate it could be fired off the trailer.

The gun was originally fitted with a most luxurious reflecting sight that incorporated a clockwork course-and-speed calculator, which, once set, kept the sight at the correct point of aim-off. Whilst an excellent sight, it was expensive and slow to manufacture, so it was later replaced by a much simpler open sight.

Having, as it were, given the soldiers a quick fix, Rheinmetall then sat down to make something rather more effective, and in time-honoured style they simply scaled up the 20mm weapon to 37mm calibre and developed a suitable round of ammunition for it. When it came to the mounting, however, they decided to adopt what was virtually a miniaturized medium gun carriage, using a platform with outriggers, carried on two two-wheeled axles that were to be removed when emplacing the mounting. The resulting weapon was three times the weight of the 20mm gun, had a slower rate of fire, and only lifted the operating ceiling by about 300m (1,000 feet). The army were not particularly impressed by it and very few were built in 1935–36.

Rheinmetall then developed a fresh mount-

ing, virtually an enlarged version of the trailer system used with the 20mm gun; this reduced the weight, and was easier and quicker into and out of action, although the ballistic performance was unchanged. Nevertheless, the heavier shell made up for that and the 3.7cm Flak 36 was to be the mainstay of light air-defence until 1945.

RUSSIA

The early days of Russian anti-aircraft artillery are shrouded in mystery; it seems probable that they acquired a few British 13-pounders and French 75mm weapons during World War One, but I can find no reliable information on the matter. The first purely Soviet design of AA gun was the 76.2mm M1931; this, it appears, was based upon a Vickers design of 75mm gun, of which a small number had been acquired, probably through an intermediary, in the late 1920s to give the Soviets some idea of contemporary foreign thoughts on the subject. The gun they then produced was a simple, reliable weapon carried on a two-wheeled mounting. This was the usual platform and outriggers, two outriggers acting as a trail-cum-towbar, and the other two folded up alongside the barrel. The platform was jacked up and wheels slipped onto stub axles, and the complete equipment was then ready for towing. Into action was simply a matter of unhooking, jacking up, removing the wheels, jacking down and laying out the four legs. It could fire a 6.35kg (14lb) shell to 9,000m (29,500ft) and, broadly speaking, seems to have been quite on a par with any other gun of its class. Certainly, large numbers were still in use into the 1940s.

However, an improvement was called for in the mid-1930s. Since the M1931 had been a new design it was merely a question of detail changes, to address various minor complaints from the customers. The mounting was turned into a four-wheeled type with two removable limbers, data transmission dials were added and direct-fire sights were provided. The change of carriage added a little weight to the travelling load, but the ballistic performance remained the same. The resulting gun went into service as the 76.2mm M1938.

At the same time, another design team had been working on a larger equipment; the appearance of the German 88m had pointed out to the Soviets that the age-old standard of 3-inch no longer applied and that aircraft were becoming more difficult targets. More reach and a bigger shell were the twin solutions to this problem, and the 85mm M1939 gun was the result. It was little more than a scaled-up version of the 76mm M1938, but is always identifiable by the slotted muzzle brake. It had the same sort of four-wheeled mounting, receiver dials for data from the predictor and, in accordance with the Soviet policy adopted in 1937

that all artillery should be capable of shooting at tanks, it was fitted with direct-fire sights and provided with armour-piercing ammunition. But the increase in size brought about a relatively small increase in performance; the M1939 gun fired a 9kg (20lb) shell to 10,800m (35,400ft).

The last of the inter-war Soviet guns was the 105mm M1934; although a mobile gun, this seems to have been employed entirely as a static defence weapon around the major cities and military installations within the Soviet Union. It is said to have fired a 14.5kg (32lb) shell to 13,300m (43,500ft), which, if true, outperformed the German 105mm gun by a considerable margin. But, looking at the small range of air-defence weapons, it does seem that the Soviets made a shrewd assessment of the likelihood of aerial attack deep into their territory, given the state of aircraft development of the

The Soviet 85mm M1939 gun was a late attempt to stiffen up their air defences. In this case the shield was often retained since the gun, like the German 88mm, was often pressed into service as an anti-tank gun.

The Soviet 37mm M1939 was a fairly obvious copy of a Bofors design. This specimen is on display at the Polish Army Museum in Warsaw.

period, and decided that the major threat was tactical air support of an invading army rather than long-range high-altitude bombing. Hence the proliferation of the 76mm weapons with field armies and the relative scarcity of the 85 and 105mm guns.

JAPAN

Japan, like Russia, seems to have assessed the realities of aerial warfare and come to the conclusion that there was nobody within striking distance who was likely to prove a threat to their air space. No Far Eastern nation had any air force worth worrying about; the only possible threat could be from Russia and there seemed no reason for Russia to make any warlike moves in their direction. Like the Russians, therefore, they concentrated on a mobile equipment that could accompany a field army and deal with tactical air support.

The standard army gun was the 75mm Type 88; the nomenclature comes from its adoption in 1928, which was 2588 in the Japanese calendar. This was a quite conventional weapon; the only oddity being that the platform had five outriggers instead of the usual four. Like most Japanese artillery it was light in relation to its power, weighing only 2.7 tons in travelling order, but it could fire a 6.3kg (14lb) shell to 7,200m (23,500ft), which was quite sufficient for its intended employment.

The only other army air-defence weapons were, firstly, a 20mm cannon on wheels, adopted in 1935, and, secondly, a 105mm gun Type 14 that dated from 1925 and which was, quite frankly, obsolete by 1939. Although half the weight of its German or Russian equivalents, it fired a 15.8kg (35lb) shell to 11,000m (36,000ft). However, there were not many of them and when the war began to make itself felt in Japan the shortage of anti-aircraft guns was to cause considerable problems.

4 The Electronic Age

FINDING THE TARGET

The use of radio waves to detect the presence of distant aircraft and so give warning of their approach appears to have occurred to a number of people at more or less the same period of time, from the late 1920s to the early 1930s. Sir Robert Watson-Watt's place as the 'father of radar' was earned not by his discovery of the phenomenon but by his percipience in seeing the overall possibilities. In effect, where the American, French and German scientists said, 'Do this and you will detect the presence of an aircraft,' Watson-Watt said, 'Do this and you will detect an aircraft; do it from two places and you will locate the aircraft; do *this* and you will determine its altitude; do *that* and you will determine its distance; feed this information to a central point and it can despatch aircraft to intercept, and by doing *this* and *that* you will be able to direct the intercepting aircraft into the path of the intruder . . .' and so on until he had virtually laid out the entire defensive plan that has more or less been followed ever since. He foresaw the effects of electronic warfare before the first radar set had even worked and, having seen the flight of heavy artillery shells fired from Brackenbury Battery close to Bawdsey on an early coast-watching radar in the summer of 1939, he was alive to the possibilities of using the system to direct artillery fire.

One thing should be made clear at the start: although we speak of 'directing gunfire' by radar, in actual fact we do no such thing. 'Directing gunfire' suggests a controller sitting at a radar screen watching the approaching bomber and also watching the bursting shells as they reflect the radar signals, after which he does a quick calculation and shouts 'Left a bit! Add two hundred!' to the waiting guns. Not so. What the radar does is to say where the target is and keep up a running commentary on its position, course and speed. This information then goes into the predictor, to be incorporated in its mathematics, and the resulting data are passed to the guns for them to fire. At no stage of the business is there any attempt to correlate the position of the aircraft and the position of the bursting shells. It is as well to dispose of this now, so that no misapprehensions can arise due to building up a mental picture on a false premise. (I fell into this trap myself some fifty years ago, on my first introduction to air-defence radar; as a field gunner I could not, at first, imagine a system of gunnery devoid of visual observation and control.)

The story of radar has been told many times and is now well-known, but the story as usually told is devoted entirely to its use in detecting oncoming aircraft and directing interception by fighters, and then to its use by bomber aircraft to find their targets and navigate. Army radar, which includes not only anti-aircraft gun control but also field and coast artillery fire direction and the detection of hostile mortars, is dealt with cursorily, if at all. And yet the Royal Artillery had a liaison officer attached to the first experimental laboratory at Bawdsey Manor and were investigating its applications to gunnery from 1936 onward. But since, as we have seen, early warning was as vital to gunnery as it was to aircraft interception, the priority in the early days was correctly placed on the early warning and reporting system, and the more direct application to gunnery was treated solely from the theoretical point of view, against the day when some practical work could be started.

But before we explore the impact of electronics on air defence, it would be salutary to start our study of fire control in the 1920s, for only by appreciating the problem as it was then seen can you appreciate the relief when the solution was found.

As we have previously noted, the only method of alerting the defences of the approach of an aircraft was a combination of ground watchers and sound detection, and this had become a viable system by 1918. The weak link in the system was sound detection; the problem was primarily one for the air forces, because they needed sufficient warning to be able to fly their aircraft off the ground and up to an operational height before the bombers reached them, a process that could take anything up to twenty minutes. This was also the factor that governed the proposed disposition of guns in various air-defence schemes proposed in the 1920s: assuming that the first

warning would come from sound detectors on the English coast and that subsequent reports would come from ground observers, the fighter aircraft had to be stationed sufficiently far inland for them to take off and reach their desired height in the time available. Therefore the gap between the coastline and the aircraft fighting-zone was the property of the air-defence guns.

But the unfortunate and awkward fact was that the sound-detecting equipment available at the end of the war was only capable of extending the detection range by about 50 per cent more than that of the unaided human ear – from about 4 miles to about 6 miles on a good day seemed to be the average gain. And 6 miles at 150mph was 2.4 minutes, barely enough time to get a gun laid and loaded, let alone get an aeroplane off the ground.

As with many wartime innovations, peacetime brought the chance to do some more fundamental research and either improve the device or show it to be impractical. And so it

The US Army Sound Detector M1 of 1938 used four horns to give approximate direction and elevation data.

*The British Sound
Detector of the same
period also used four horns,
but whether round horns
showed any improvement
over square ones, or vice
versa, is not clear.*

was with sound detection; more research went into the subject and some basic facts were accumulated, one of them being that the parabolic mirror was more reliable and sensitive than the 'ear trumpet' style, and another being that the mirror needed to be of some dense material that would reflect sound and not absorb it.

A scientist named Tucker, who worked for the Air Defence Experimental Establishment and was an expert on acoustics, was the principal champion of the sound mirror and constructed a 20-foot diameter parabolic concrete mirror on the downs above Romney Marsh in Kent, oriented towards France – which, at that time, was considered to be the only possible threat. A pole in front of the mirror indicated the focal point and, initially, a form of medical stethoscope was fixed there to detect the sounds reflected from the mirror. Later this was replaced by elec-

trical microphones, which could be rotated and tilted so as to focus on various parts of the mirror surface, from which the direction of the sound could be calculated with reasonable accuracy.

The 20ft (6m) mirror was reasonably successful, lifting the detection range to 10 or more miles on a good day; for the system was increasingly affected by weather, meteorological conditions such as air density and vapour content, and, of course, by extraneous noise. It was found on flying trials, for example, that the noise of one of 'our' aircraft on a routine patrol could drown out any sound of 'their' aircraft approaching over a wide area.

Nevertheless, it was, as they say, the only game in town and Tucker pressed on with his researches. His next step was a number of 30ft (9m) parabolic mirrors, and then a 200ft (60m)

The sound mirror above Romney Marsh, seen in 1978. The spindle in the centre of the mirror carried two microphones and could be moved to detect sound from various directions within the compass of the mirror.

long mirror, 36ft (11m) high, and curved along its length, with a series of microphones across its focal points. This could detect approaching aircraft at over 20 miles when conditions were right and, by the early 1930s, the government of the day were coming round to the idea of spending a very large sum of money on a series of 200-foot mirrors along the south-east coast, when everything had to be halted. The accession of Adolf Hitler suddenly transposed the threat direction; instead of the bombers coming across Kent from France, they would now be coming across Norfolk from Germany. This led to what was known as the 'Re-Orientation Plan', moving the planned defensive areas for guns and fighter aircraft from the south-east to East Anglia, and land agents and surveyors began scouring Essex and Sussex for sites for the 200-foot mirrors to be oriented against Germany.

It will be recalled that in 1918 General Ashmore had built up a system of observers –

Rear view of the Romney mirror; the sheep in front give an idea of its size.

police and military – across East Anglia, through which any enemy aircraft was reported to a central control room that then alerted guns and aircraft on the estimated path of the raiders. In 1924, by which time Ashmore was Inspector of Anti-Aircraft, he was asked to investigate the possibility of building up a similar system across the entire country, starting in the east and south-east of England where the threat was most obvious. In the next six years, from a start using three observing posts and trial flights by single aircraft, he put together a complex network of observers, linked to local control centres, which in turn were linked into the general air-defence system. It was almost entirely a volunteer, part-time force, manned by civilians, policemen, ex-service men and Boy Scouts and, by participation in RAF exercises, soon attained a high standard of proficiency, and in the course of time was regularized as the Observer Corps. It served so well during World War Two that it became the Royal Observer Corps in recognition of the vital role it had played.

While all this was going on, the smaller-scale problem of what to do once you had warning and details of approaching aircraft was also being tackled. There was no argument about what was wanted; course, speed and altitude of the aircraft on the one hand, velocity and ballistic coefficient of the shell on the other. Air density, wind direction and speed, humidity, temperature of the gun propellant and a few other measurable quantities were also desirable for a complete and accurate computation, the end result of which would be an azimuth, an elevation and a fuze length to be transmitted to the gun. Given all the necessary figures, a pencil and a slide rule, any good mathematician could produce the solution but by the time he did so the bomber would probably be on its way home again. The problem was handed to the scientific instrument makers.

The wartime Central Post Instruments and Brocq Tachymeters had shown the way – use voltages and currents to represent values, gears and differentials to add and subtract, divide and multiply. Using these as a starting point, companies like Metropolitan Vickers, Sperry Gyroscopes, Siemens, Telefunken and Zeiss set their scientists to work to produce computing machines of considerable complexity. Known

Once past the mirror, or the later coast radar, tracking of a raider depended entirely on members of the Observer Corps.

variously as 'predictors' in Britain, 'directors' in the USA and *Kommandogerät* in Germany, they all finished up looking very much the same and operating in very much the same manner. They all incorporated a telescope, for tracking the target, and this was converted into an angular velocity. A rangefinder provided range and height and this, fed into the predictor, interacted with the angular velocity to give the target's course and speed. Meteorological conditions, measured locally, were set on dials and the predictor was (in today's terms) 'programmed' with the ballistic details of the gun with which it was working. It now calculated a forward position for the aircraft, then worked out an elevation, azimuth and fuze-length for the gun, determined where that would burst the shell and compared it with the 'future position' of the target. If the two differed, a fresh solution was tried until agreement was reached and the results displayed on dials for transmission to the guns, either (in the early days) by shouting or telephone, later by automatic electrical transmission to dials on the guns.

This was a continuous process, following the target and constantly updating the 'future position' and consequently the gun data. And since there was no observation of the burst of the shell and no corrections based upon it, there was no waiting for results before firing the next round. The gun layers pointed the gun in accordance with the dials and as soon as the target was within range the gun commenced firing and continued to fire as fast as possible, the layers constantly laying against the fresh settings of the dials, until either they scored a hit or the target flew out of range.

This sort of on-going calculation demanded some complex machinery; some of it could be represented by electricity, much of it not.

Members of the Auxiliary Territorial Service (the female element of the British Army during World War Two) operating a predictor for a battery of 4.5-inch guns.

The result was that the predictor became a heavy and expensive device. The German Kommandogerät 36 required thirteen men to operate it, while the replacement, the KG40, contained thirty-five differentials and twenty-four electric motors and weighed 1.5 tons. The American Sperry T8 of 1937 contained no less than 3,500 separate components. In time, and with the introduction of more electrical and electronic components the size and weight came down, but they were still large devices. They

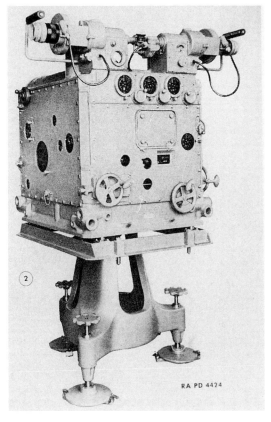

The US Director M7A1B2 was probably the ultimate in electro-mechanical predictors. Weighing 960lbs (435kg) without its pedestal, it required eight operators and could cope with targets flying at 410mph (660km/h) at altitudes up to 33,000ft (10,000m).

were also improved by separating some of the functions so as to reduce the size of the predictor and, more importantly, reduce the number of operators elbowing each other out of the way. So the height finder, the rangefinder, the tracker, all became separate instruments, connected electrically to the predictor and transmitting continuous data to it.

All this was well on the way to a reliable and trustworthy condition by the middle 1930s. All the system now needed was sufficient early warning to get the men on to the instruments and guns and have everything running sweetly as the target hove into view. And there, at that point, came the final complication. If the target hove into view on a fine clear day, all was well; if it chose to turn up when the sky was covered in cloud, or in a snowstorm, or fog, or at night, the whole system collapsed, because it was entirely dependent upon being able to track the target visually. At night searchlights could be used, but they had to find the target themselves to begin with before they could illuminate it for the tracking instruments. In good daylight and with fair weather, the anti-aircraft gunner stood a good chance of making life very uncomfortable for the target; at night, or in poor weather, he stood very little chance at all.

But sound was not the only detection system being pursued. Several prominent scientists had their doubts about acoustic methods and preferred to put their money on another contender, infra-red detection – detecting the heat emitted by an aircraft's engine.

Infra-red detection had first been put forward during World War One, though not in the air-defence context; at that stage of its development, the range at which temperature anomalies could be detected was far too short to be able to detect aircraft, and the principal proposal was to use it to detect night raids by infantry across No Man's Land. German scientists also developed a detector that, deployed on the Belgian coast, could pick up British motor-torpedo-boats operating close to the shore at night.

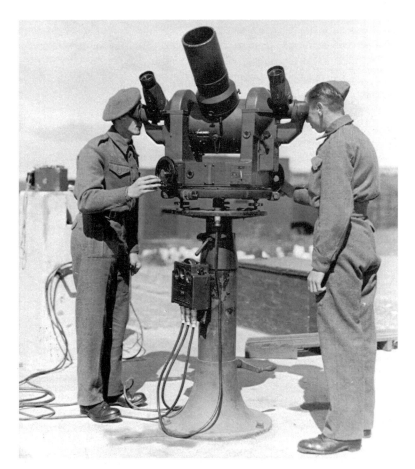

An optical tracker being used to feed information to a predictor. Two men are necessary, one tracking for direction, the other for height.

Nothing much came of the work during the war, but scientific interest had been roused and work continued in the 1920s on developing detectors that gave promise of being able to identify targets at aircraft ranges, and by the early 1930s some startling results were being achieved. An American scientist, Dr Harold Zahl, developed a multiple thermocouple apparatus, using a 60in (1.5m) parabolic searchlight mirror as a reflecting surface, capable of detecting a twin-engined bomber at 20,000 yards (18km) range and tracking it with sufficient accuracy to be able to direct a searchlight to illuminate when the target was 12,000 yards (11km) away.

The principal drawback was that cloud cover damped out the temperature difference and it was thus impossible to detect or track an aircraft above the clouds. The credit side of infrared, of course, was its ability to work in complete darkness as well as, if not better than, in daylight. It is interesting to note that, during the early days of American radar, infra-red was combined with radar, since radar could detect at long ranges but was incapable of measuring direction as accurately as infra-red.

Much work was done with infra-red in Britain and, by the mid-1930s, there was considerable rivalry between the supporters of sound detection and the infra-red enthusiasts. It was into this situation that radar suddenly appeared and, if the scientists were to be believed, promised to solve all the problems at once: it would provide early warning up to 50 or more miles distant; it would provide continuous tracking in any weather, by day or by night; it would give an instant position at any time; and it could feed the predictor with all the information that had, hitherto, been provided by two or three different instruments, all of which contained their own degree of error. Heaven was just around the corner for the ack-ack gunner; or so it seemed.

In fact, and in retrospect, Britain came late to the radar scene, and one can only assume that scarcity of money, leading to a scarcity of scientific minds in government service, caused the delay. For the principle of reflecting radio waves was known, and used for ionospheric research, and the refinement of using pulses of radio energy, alternating with periods of transmission silence so that the returning echo could be detected, was also well understood. Research into using this technique to locate aerial targets began in the USA in 1931 at the Signal Corps Laboratory in Fort Monmouth, New Jersey. It began in Germany in 1934 with Dr Kühnhold of the Germany Naval Radio Research Establishment making experiments based upon published reports of the ionospheric researches then being conducted. In France a group of scientists was developing a system for detecting icebergs at sea, with the intention of fitting it to their transatlantic liners to avoid another *Titanic* disaster. But Britain, though starting relatively late, made up for it in the high quality of subsequent research and development and because, as already said, the whole air-defence system tied to the radar was foreseen and developed as a complete system, so that a defensive screen was in place by the autumn of 1938 and has been maintained ever since.

The initial impetus – and the money – for the first steps in British radar had come from the Royal Air Force, and, hardly surprisingly, their requirements were the first priority. But in 1936 a small artillery team was installed at Bawdsey Manor, where the first research laboratories were set up, with the task of developing a radar set suitable for providing early warning of the approach of enemy aircraft, with azimuth and range of sufficient accuracy to be able to point optical instruments, such as height finders and trackers, so as to pick up individual targets. Their task was not made any easier by the demand that, since the equipment was to provide information for mobile medium anti-aircraft guns, then it too had to be mobile and compact and easy to set up, and easy to operate, and cheap, and easy to manufacture, and simple to maintain . . . all the desiderata which were invariably trotted out when any new piece of equipment was proposed.

The first prototype of a 'gun-laying' (GL) radar appeared in 1937, and demonstrated a range of 20,000 yards (18.3km or 11.3 miles). More work went into the design and in 1938 it was approved for production as the GL1 set. Sets began reaching the hands of gun regiments late in 1939 and by the summer of 1940 some 425 sets had been produced and put into service. In order to meet the mobility requirement the GL1 came in two separate units, the transmitter and the receiver, each on a four-wheeled trailer. The cumbersome antenna arrays had to be assembled and fitted to the cabin roof once the trailer had been positioned, the two units connected and generators connected – a fairly slow and precise process. Once in action the set could detect a target to a range of about 30,000 yards (27.5km) with an accuracy of plus or minus 25 yards (23m). The whole cabin, with its antenna, could be revolved on the trailer to give directional coverage and it was possible to estimate direction to an accuracy of about 2 or 3 degrees. This was far from the accuracy required to direct gunfire, but it was good enough to point optical instruments in the right direction so as to acquire the target visually. It followed, therefore, that at night or in poor visibility, the set could only be relied upon for early warning.

The answer to the accuracy problem was known in theory but difficult to achieve in practice, for the scientists working on the development of radar were exploring an entirely new field and were having to discover the rules as they went along. In simple terms, the problem was that the radar set of 1940 was like a floodlight, spreading its emission over a wide area and reflecting from whatever it found. Direction could only be ascertained by swinging the 'light' from side to side and seeing at what point the reflection was most bright. Elevation could have been achieved the same way but for the fact that the antenna array was far too cumbersome to be swung up and down. The reason for the cumbersome antenna was that the best results were achieved with an aerial rod half the wavelength of the emitted signal. To obtain a shorter wavelength was relatively easy but not at the power demanded; the set had to send out a pulse capable of travelling up to 100 miles and then pick up the echo – at a strength estimated by a contemporary writer as being about one millionth of one millionth of the emitted signal. So in order to get a usable echo, you needed a powerful initial pulse. Power was a product of the vacuum tubes used in the set; here the designers were working at the extreme front-edge of their technology and not obtaining as much power as they would like. Because not only did power mean range, power at a shorter wavelength, for reasons we need not enter into here, meant a smaller antenna, which meant an antenna which could be moved about more easily to obtain direction and elevation. And as the wavelength got shorter, so the 'beam of light' shrank until the floodlight became a spotlight. The ultimate object of this research was a thin pencil-beam capable of picking out a target with the utmost precision.

In fact, the American experimenters in this field had begun by specifying a wavelength of 9cm, and had successfully detected targets at a range of a few hundred yards, but the amount of power they could transmit was derisory and there was no prospect of improving matters, so they dropped the idea and went for a lower fre-

quency and longer wavelength, simply to get more range.

BRITAIN

With radar early-warning and optical tracking once the target was within range, daylight air defence in good weather was reasonably successful in the opening year of the war; where it did not actually bring raiders down, it kept them at a respectable distance and broke up formations so as to make individual targets available to fighter aircraft. Where visibility prevented optical tracking, attempts to rely entirely upon radar information led to a few embarrassing moments; such as the incident on 6 September 1939, when radar indications showed a serious attack threat from aircraft approaching across the North Sea. Fighters were flown off to intercept. More raiders appeared. More fighters took off. An hour later, after three RAF aircraft had been lost, the awful truth emerged: there were no enemy raiders. The initial sighting had been of RAF aircraft on a simple training flight somewhere over Hampshire, but by an anomaly or some human error the bearing was read 180 degrees wrong. The fighters that took off were plotted in the wrong area, adding to the apparent number of raiders, thus generating more fighters, which added to the numbers . . . A gun battery in the Thames estuary opened up and destroyed a twin-engined bomber, which, unfortunately, was an RAF Blenheim, while two Hurricanes were shot down when two fighter squadrons met. The whole affair went down in air defence history as the 'Battle of Barking Creek' and was to become the awful warning of what could happen if things went wrong.

Guns made their first score of World War Two on 4 September 1939, when the RAF attacked the heavy cruiser *Admiral Scheer* and the cruiser *Emden* in the Heligoland Bight. Due to poor weather conditions the nineteen

The British 3-inch 20cwt gun in its final mobile form, with pneumatic tyres. Not the least interesting feature is the rifle rack, carefully positioned to receive the spray and dirt from the wheels of the towing vehicle.

August 1938, the Munich Crisis, and a 3-inch 20cwt is positioned on Westminster Bridge, London, to protect the Houses of Parliament. Photograph by courtesy of Major Julian Pearce, RA, who was the sergeant in charge of the gun.

attacking bombers had to go in at minimum height, well within the range of even the 20mm guns with which both ships were liberally equipped. As a result, seven aircraft were shot down, an inauspicious beginning for Bomber Command's operations.

The turn of the British gunners did not come until the following month, since the Luftwaffe were slower in starting their bombing campaign. But on 16 October a number of German aircraft swept up the Firth of Forth making for two warships close to the Forth Bridge. A gun battery on the south side of the Forth was engaged in gun drill when the alert was sounded and, rapidly discarding dummy ammunition for live, they engaged the raiders and shot away part of the tail of one Heinkel He 111 bomber. It limped away to be finished off by a Spitfire, so the first German aircraft to be brought down over Britain was a combined affair by both arms of the defences.

The 'Sitzkrieg' or 'Phoney War' was finally ended by the German attacks on Norway and Denmark, and then the advance into the Low Countries and France in May 1940. The propagators of the cataclysmic theory of bombing found new support for their fears on 14 May when the Luftwaffe bombed Rotterdam. The bombing was accompanied by an artillery bombardment and the damage and casualties were severe, but the confused conditions of the time ensured that the tale lost nothing in its telling and, taken together with pseudo-nuns descending by parachute, lady hikers in jackboots and similar rumours, served to sharpen apprehensions of an airborne attack on Britain.

In spite of the factories turning out guns during the winter months, the defences were, in fact, little better than they had been on 3 September. Guns had to be sent to France with the British Expeditionary Force, and the greatest absorber of armament was an insatiable Royal Navy who, in their role as Senior Service, took good care to seize the lion's share of any weapons that were available. In December 1939

they demanded 255 guns to protect fleet anchorages, at a time when the London area had only ninety-six guns and a target of such vital importance as the Rolls-Royce aero-engine factory had but eight guns to protect it. Although the overall command of the air defence of Great Britain was in the capable hands of Air Marshal Dowding, and the AA Artillery under General Pile, neither were consulted as to the allocation of gun defences, which was now in the hands of the Deputy Chiefs-of-Staff Committee, some of whose decisions defied rational explanation. In January the Admiralty suggested sending all the 3.7-inch guns in Britain to France to replace the 3-inch guns of the BEF, these 3-inch then being sent back to Britain and presented to the Royal Navy. Such a move would have practically stripped Britain of what defences there were, but fortunately it was scotched by the BEF refusing to have the 3.7-inch guns; they preferred their more manoeuvrable 3-inch guns for mobile warfare.

The lack of light guns – in March 1940 there were only 108 Bofors guns in the whole of the United Kingdom – led to a wholesale issue of obsolescent Lewis light machine guns; they were relatively useless apart from their value in raising morale by allowing the troops to shoot back. Over 3,000 of these were issued, with makeshift mountings, but in February 1940 the Navy demanded 800 of them, raised their demand to 1,300 in the following month, and then asked for another 1,600, which would have effectively removed the Lewis gun from the land defences by midsummer.

While this was still being argued the German invasion of Norway took place, resulting in a fresh Admiralty demand for another 800 Lewis guns in order to arm Norwegian and Danish merchant ships, plus a demand from the planning staff of the War Office for 144 heavy and 144 light guns to be sent to Norway forthwith. This was patently impossible; it was thought that, at most, ninety-five guns of all types could

A Bofors gun in action. An unusual picture because in front of the gun is a predictor and crew and there are no gun layers on the gun. This must have been an early remote power-operated design under trial.

be made available by cutting Britain's defences to the bone, but before that step could be taken it became obvious that Norway was a lost cause and the demand was cancelled.

In July 1940, with the Army recovering its breath after Dunkirk, a quick stock-check revealed the gun strength in Britain to be 1,280 medium (3.7-inch and 4.5-inch) and 517 light (2-pounder, 3-inch and 40mm). This may sound reasonable until the figures are compared with the strengths actually planned: 3,744 medium, 4,410 light and over 8,000 rocket projectors, resulting in a total deficiency of 2,464 medium, 3,993 light and over 8,000 rocket projectors. There was a long way to go. But before much else could be done the Luftwaffe at last began the all-out attack on Britain that had been so confidently expected in the previous September.

Much has been written about the Battle of Britain and there is doubtless more to come,

though recent tendency appears to lean towards disputing whether it ever happened and, if so, who won. I know it happened, since much of it took place over my head, but I was not, at that time, privy to the higher councils, so no searching analysis of motives and actions need be expected here. Indeed it must be dealt with relatively briefly, since it was but one facet of the history of air defence, but it was a facet which revealed the wisdom of some aspects of pre-war planning and also some of the weaknesses; while the Battle of Britain certainly saved the country in 1940, it is equally certain that by focusing everyone's eyes on air attacks and the necessity for defence, and thus accelerating the development and production of equipment, it went a long way towards building up the defensive apparatus that was to save the south of England from near-certain destruction in 1944.

The first German moves came in the form of

increasing attacks on coastal areas, Dover in particular being a frequent target – the guns there achieving considerable success. One result of this sudden increase in activity was that guns in the coastal area were having to be manned for twenty-four hours a day, and this sort of demand had not been envisaged by those who had planned the manpower structure of an anti-aircraft battery; the scale of manpower had been based upon the World War One experience of short bursts of activity in daylight, with infrequent activity at night, a regime that allowed the men to sleep, eat, maintain their guns, fetch ammunition and so forth. But the constant alerts, together with the other domestic day-to-day demands left little time to eat or sleep and units were threatened with the prospect of coming to a standstill out of sheer fatigue. In the worst cases it was found necessary to draft more men in and double the pre-war strength of a battery so as to provide enough officers and men to operate a non-stop shift system.

The observing and reporting network set up by General Ashmore now began to show its worth, as did the infant radar network. By this time the radar system stretched in an unbroken barrier from the Isle of Wight to the Orkneys and from a range of over 100 miles the stations were able to see the assembly of German aircraft into raiding formations over their French airfields, track them and alert the defenders, so that when the raiders closed with the English coast they found a suitable force of fighters, well disposed tactically, waiting to deal with them. The only defect, at the beginning, was the inability of the radar operators to estimate the strength of the incoming raids, since they had not had the opportunity of seeing such quantities of aircraft on their screens before, but that sort of error soon became a thing of the past as, with more practice, operators soon became uncannily accurate at assessing numbers from the appearance of the echo signals on their screen.

It is also worth making the point that the radar system as it stood in 1940 was a single line of stations running down the east coast of Britain and oriented to look eastwards. Once an enemy aircraft flew over the top of the radar station, it was lost to the radar, and its subsequent tracking was down to the Observer Corps.

By this time the Germans had realized that some form of radio detection was in use, though since their own system was at an early stage of development they had no inkling of the immense scope of the British network. On 12 August, therefore, came a systematic attack on five radar stations, from Dunkirk in Kent to Ventnor on the Isle of Wight. They were glaringly obvious targets, with aerial masts towering 300 and more feet above them, but they were singularly difficult to put out of action except by complete destruction. Within six hours of the attack all except one was back in operation, the exception being Ventnor, which had had a scattering of delayed-action bombs and had to be evacuated until these could be dealt with. A mobile set, which had been designed for just such an emergency, was set up and filled the gap.

On the day after this attack, the German raiders were greeted by RAF fighters in the customary fashion, from which the Luftwaffe concluded that there was no profit in attacking radar stations; yet had these attacks been followed up in systematic fashion, putting the stations out of action day after day, there is little doubt that the warning system would have been severely reduced in its efficiency. But the quick rebound of these first stations gave an impression of impervious omniscience that did the trick.

The attack then turned to fighter stations, ten of Fighter Command's eleven fields being bombed and machine-gunned on 13 August while the radar stations were untouched. Again, had this line of attack been followed up the consequences would have been extremely serious, but again the plan was abandoned for something else. The reasons for this change were many, but particularly significant was the rate of attrition of German bombers because their escorting fighters were reaching the limit of their operational range. Once the scene of action moved further inland from Kent, the escorting fighters had to turn about and head for home, otherwise they were liable to run out of fuel, and the bombers were highly vulnerable once the escort was gone; on 15 August the Luftwaffe lost seventy-five aircraft. On that night, though, the bombers returned under cover of darkness, bombed, and went home unscathed, and after considering the implications of this, the Luftwaffe gradually swung its main effort into night raiding. The daylight attacks continued, for they were part and parcel of the *Sealion* plan to invade England, which depended on the Luftwaffe attaining air superiority over the English Channel, but on 7 September the German tactics took a new turn as 350 bombers, escorted by over 600 fighters, roared up the Thames estuary late in the afternoon. Assuming another attack on the fighter stations, the RAF controllers had deployed their forces accordingly, so that only a relatively weak screen of fighters covered the route to London. These were soon swept aside by the massive escort; London's dockland was set ablaze, while the Germans lost ten bombers and twenty-two fighters to the RAF's twenty-nine fighters lost. The blazing Thames-side acted as a beacon for a fresh force of 318 bombers, which appeared over the target shortly after 10.00pm and, free of interference, systematically pounded London until 4.30am. The following day saw heroic efforts by the London Fire Brigade, but many fires were still burning as night fell and they marked the way for a fresh attack. The Blitz had begun, and it was to continue for sixty-five successive nights.

While the defences had been well pleased with their performance during the August–September day battles, the change to night attacks soon put their feet back on the ground. The inadequate defence of London by guns and the inability of fighters to find targets at night were both revealed in the most violent manner. Within forty-eight hours the gun strength was increased to 371 barrels by bringing in guns from all over Britain, but even this addition had little effect; in the first four nights only four aircraft were brought down by gunfire. The most noticeable thing to Londoners, though, was that while there seemed to be a lot more guns around the place, there didn't seem to be much increase in the amount of firing going on, and some gun sites were observed not to fire at all during raids. There was a good deal of criticism of the AA defences on this score, but what the public failed to appreciate was that in several cases the guns were silenced in order to let RAF fighters have a free run.

Nevertheless, much of the trouble stemmed from the fire control system in use, an extension of the pre-war fixed azimuth system. This relied on a network of mobile sound-locators, which had been installed just before the war when it was apparent that army radar was at a low priority. This system produced a predicted path of the raid based on those aircraft that appeared more or less on the centre of the listening zone; from this a future position was deduced and passed to the guns on the raid track, which then opened fire. But it meant that raiders that, by luck or good judgement, evaded the sound locators were not predicted and the guns in their path, in the absence of any data, were unable to open fire.

On 10 September, General Pile, commanding the gun defences, decided to abandon what he termed 'the precise inaccuracies of the fixed azimuth system'. He called a meeting of the commanders of every gun position in and around London and gave instructions that henceforth all guns would fire every possible round, pointing at an approximate bearing and elevation based on whatever information the site commander could obtain and on his

educated guess if nothing better was available. No searchlights would expose and no RAF aircraft would enter the area; everything that flew was to be fired at without question or hesitation. Not only would defences be operating, they would be seen and heard to be operating.

> The result was as astonishing to me as it appears to have been to the citizens of London – and, apparently, to the enemy as well. For, although few of the bursts could have been anywhere near the target, the heights of aircraft steadily increased as the night went on, and many of them turned away before entering the Inner Artillery Zone . . . it was in no sense a barrage, though I think by that it will always be known . . .
>
> (*General Sir Frederick Pile:* Ack-Ack)

While the citizens of Central London were ecstatic at the noise and fury of the guns, those in the outlying suburbs were less enchanted, due to the number of bombs jettisoned at random by the raiders. General Pile recorded one of the many complaints which reached his office in the next few days: 'The council of an outer suburb wrote to say that council house lavatory pans were being cracked by gun vibration and could we please move the barrage somewhere else.' But on the whole, the 'barrage' was a popular move until people began to realize that there seemed to be very few crashed aircraft as a result of all the noise.

It was not an easy life for the gunners. *Roof over Britain*, an official account of AA published in 1943 by the Ministry of Information, recorded the experience of a battery brought into the London area from the Humber defences. Within twenty-five hours of receiving orders to move, it had arrived in London and had to begin by clearing a bomb-blasted site of rubble in order to provide a gun area. By 7.30pm the guns were ready; at 8.15pm they went into action until 6.00am next morning. The guns were then cleaned, ammunition stocks replenished, and the gunners went to bed at 9.30am, to be roused thirty minutes later by a daylight alert. The gunners continued this routine for eight days, 'with so little sleep that at times the gun layers were almost unconscious as they tried to keep their eyes focused on the dials'. On the ninth day the men were relieved by a battery of recent recruits who had never fired the guns before and had to be given a quick course of instruction before they could be left in charge.

The balloon aprons of 1918 had been revived in a different form in 1936, when the Air Staff laid plans for a ring of balloons around London, without the connecting apron, spaced at about ten balloons to the mile and requiring 450 balloons. This plan was rapidly changed when it was realized that a ring of balloons merely forced an attacker to fly high in order to cross the ring, after which he could come down to bombing height once more, and 'field siting', an irregular pattern all over the area, was adopted.

By the spring of 1941 radar began to appear in serviceable form and usable quantity; in ground control interception sets, which allowed RAF controllers to track raiders and fighters and command the fighters, by voice radio, into the area of the enemy; in airborne intercept sets carried in fighters, which allowed them to make contact in the dark; and in GL2 sets, which could provide the AA predictors with accurate information on the target height, range and bearing. The GL2 sets at first displayed some peculiar aberrations, which were eventually traced to irregular signal reflections from the surrounding ground. This was cured by laying a flat screen of chicken wire around the set to give an artificial plane from which the signals could reflect in an orderly manner. Even this seemingly simple solution raised problems; it demanded some 480km (300 miles) of chicken wire, all there was in the country, and there were many people who, intent upon keeping a few chickens to augment their rations, were somewhat baffled to find that such a peaceful commodity had vanished from the market.

One of the most serious gaps in the defences of London was the River Thames itself; it lay like a directional sign pointing the way to the capital, and its mouth was so wide that guns positioned at either side could not bar the entrance. In 1941 the Admiralty became concerned with this gap since it was being exploited not only by bombers but also by mine-laying aircraft, and they invited a Mr G. A. Maunsell, a noted civil engineer, to consider the construction of some sort of artificial island upon which anti-aircraft guns could be mounted.

Artificial sea forts were no novelty in British defences; they had been built in Plymouth and Portsmouth harbours in the 1870s and in the Humber estuary during World War One, but these structures had taken years to build on their selected sites, a course which was obviously impractical in this case since the first sign of construction activity would invite attention from the Luftwaffe. Maunsell therefore proposed building the forts in dry dock, complete

The Radar GL2, showing the chicken-wire 'artificial ground-level' allowing accurate elevations to be determined.

in every detail, then towing them out to their location and there sinking them to rest on the sea bed.

Each fort consisted of a boat-like concrete pontoon 168ft (51.2m) long, 88ft (26.8m) wide and 14ft (4.2m) deep, on top of which rose two cylindrical concrete towers 24ft (7.3m) in diameter and 60ft (18.3m) high. On top of these towers was a four-decked steel superstructure to accommodate a crew of 120 men, two 3.7-inch and two Bofors 40mm guns, together with radar, searchlights, living quarters, kitchens, and every other adjunct necessary to make each fort a self-contained unit.

Once the fort was built, it was manned in dry dock by its crew, who then familiarized them-

selves with the equipment and put the fort into commission, after which the dock was flooded. The fort now floated on the concrete pontoon and, when wind and tide were right, it was towed into place by tugs, accompanied by minesweepers and an anti-aircraft frigate to protect the operation. On reaching the site the pontoon was flooded, and in fifteen seconds the fort had sunk until the pontoon was sitting on the seabed, with the tops of the towers and the superstructure above the waterline. In one case enemy aircraft appeared within minutes of the operation being completed and the fort went straight into action.

Three Maunsell Forts were built and were located on the Tongue Sand, north of Margate, Knock John, off the Essex coast, and Sunk Head, near Clacton-on-Sea. Shortly after their inception the War Office obtained Mr Maunsell's services to design a different pattern of fort to be sited to cover the Thames and the Mersey estuaries. These forts used a concrete base surmounted by four hollow concrete legs holding a two-floored steel superstructure. These units were taken out to their locations by tugs and sunk in patterns in which a central unit was surrounded by six others, after which the individual units were joined by footbridges. The central tower carried the radar and predictor, while of the ring of six, four held 3.7-inch guns, one a 40mm Bofors for local defence, and one a searchlight. Three of these combinations were built across the mouth of the Mersey, known simply as Mersey 1, 2 and 3, and these were followed by three more in the middle of the Thames estuary, off the Isle of Sheppey, known as Forts U5, U6 and U7. They effectively corked the approaches to both London and Liverpool and proved of considerable value in barring the raiders' path.

Another improvement in the defences came in 1941 with the widespread adoption of Searchlight Control (SLC) radar sets which were actually mounted on the searchlight and, with an accuracy of about 2 degrees, enabled searchlights to switch on and illuminate the target without having to sweep all over the sky relying upon luck. Later versions of the SLC radar allowed the searchlight to track the target automatically once it had been locked on to it.

So far as the guns went, there was surprisingly little change; one reason for this was simply that the factories had quite enough to do in providing the requisite number of guns and replacing losses, without spending too much time on thinking about new models. But by 1942 most of the shortfall had been made up and the army could begin getting rid of its obsolete 3-inch guns, replacing them with 3.7-inch. The first stage in improvement came with the adoption of full power-control of elevation and traverse on the static 3.7-inch guns, accompanied by a new generation of predictors that could cope with faster and higher-flying targets and could accept

data directly from radar sets. These features combined to produce a smoothly tracking, rapidly moving, medium gun and this, in its turn, showed up the slow rate of fire due to hand loading, which had been concealed when the guns were manually operated. A 'Machine, Fuze Setting, No 11' was developed and fitted to the 3.7-inch static mounting, which almost doubled the rate of fire. Similar to those described with the German guns, the MFS11 used a rocking tray to convey the complete round to the fuze setter, withdraw it, swing it into line with the breech and then ram the round home. The tray swung clear as the breech closed and the gun fired automatically. All the gunners had to do was keep the tray supplied.

The addition of the MFS to the gun also improved the accuracy, something that the layman might find peculiar. The reason for this

A fully power-operated 3.7-inch gun required only one man, the 'Number One' on the mounting, to fire the initial round and make all safe after the last round. The remainder of the detachment merely threw ammunition into the loading tray as fast as they could.

The static 3.7-inch Mark 2C mounting with the Machine, Fuze Setting, No 11 and all its accessories.

A closer view of the MFS11. The actual fuze setter is the square box above and to the right of the trunnion. Behind it is the underside of the loading tray, folded up and riding on the rods that allow it to move forward with a loaded round and set the fuze. The tray then returned to the position you see now, thus dumping the round into the second tray, from where it was rammed.

Rear view of the 3.7-inch Mark 2C showing the loading and ramming trays of the MFS11.

was that the loading sequence now took a definite fixed amount of time and was not a variable that depended upon the strength and fitness of the gunner loading the breech. And in the calculation performed by the predictor, the calculated fuze length was based upon the time of flight of the shell from the instant of firing to the instant of arriving at the future position of the target. Therefore an allowance had to be added to that timing to cater for the delay between actually setting the fuze and firing the shell. With hand loading, this was a variable, and therefore an average 'dead time' figure was incorporated into the calculation. But with the whole thing done by a machine an absolutely accurate dead time could now be applied, and this had its effect on the accuracy of the bursting shell.

The ammunition was improved by the adoption of a mechanical time-fuze as standard. This was not only more accurate but it also allowed for a longer running time than had been possible with a combustion fuze, and this lifted the effective ceiling; in the case of the 3.7-inch gun it went from 7,200m to 9,650m (23,600ft to 31,700ft) with the No 2 predictor, and was later lifted again to 10,500m (34,500ft) with a later model predictor. The performance of the 4.5-inch gun was almost the same, since even though it fired a heavier shell the velocity was slightly less than that of the 3.7-inch gun and it used similar fuzes.

The Bofors 40mm equipment had also undergone various improvements, though the gun itself was untouched. The four-wheeled mounting had been somewhat simplified in the interests of more rapid production; various types of sight had been tried and discarded or adopted before some new one came along. A special predictor – the Kerrison or Predictor No 3 – was developed to suit the ballistics of the gun and the SLC searchlight radar set had been successfully used to direct fire against targets concealed by low cloud or darkness.

For all that, however, AA Command were not satisfied; there were two areas of the sky where they were unable to perform effectively. Firstly, of course, there was the sky above the 9,000m (29,500ft) ceiling of the two medium guns; and secondly there was a belt of sky too high for the 40mm guns and too low for the 3.7-inch and 4.5-inch guns, because they could not traverse fast enough to catch a moving target at low altitudes. So two new equipments were needed, one a powerful medium or heavy gun to get up into the sky, and the other a light, fast-moving, fast-firing gun with more performance than the 40mm and less bulk than the 3.7-inch.

As early as January 1941 the demand was voiced for a high-altitude gun, specifying a ceiling of 50,000ft (15,250m), a time of flight to that height of thirty seconds, and the ability to fire three rounds and have the fourth loaded in twenty seconds. The ballistic experts considered these figures and suggested four possible solutions: firstly, an existing 5.25-inch naval gun; secondly, the 5.25-inch gun with the bore lined

down to 4.5-inch but still using the 5.25-inch cartridge; thirdly the 5.25-inch lined down to 3.7-inch; and fourthly the existing 4.5-inch gun lined down to 3.7-inches and firing the 4.5-inch cartridge. The 5.25-inch gun was selected as the long-term solution (for a suitable land-service mounting would have to be designed and built) and, for the interim solution, the 4.5 lined down to 3.7 would be adopted.

Since high velocity was essential, a new type of rifling was developed; known as RD (for Research Department) Rifling, it was designed by Colonel G. O. C. Probert of that Department, and it worked in conjunction with a specially designed shell. The rifling commenced at zero depth and the lands gradually assumed their full height at just over 4 inches from the chamber. Towards the muzzle the groove depth gradually reduced until at 11 inches from the muzzle, the bottom of the grooves had come up to meet the top of the lands and the gun was a smoothbore.

The shell was fitted with a high-efficiency driving band, and twin centring-bands at the shoulder. These had the effect of dividing the torsional stress of spinning more evenly along the length of the shell and centring the projectile more perfectly on the axis of the gun barrel. As the rifling grooves decreased, so the copper of the driving and centring bands was squeezed into prepared grooves in the shell body, and on leaving the muzzle, these copper bands, which normally protruded into the airstream and degraded the shell's flight, were smoothed flush with the shell wall to permit an unbroken air flow over the shell, which helped to sustain the velocity.

This RD Rifling was highly successful and the gun was introduced in 1943 as the 3.7-inch Mk 6 gun, the construction being a 65-calibre 3.7-inch liner inserted into the jacket of a 4.5-inch Mk 2 gun, and assembled on a 4.5-inch static mounting. This fired a 12.7kg (28lb) shell at 1,044m/sec (3,425ft/sec) to a maximum ceiling of 19,450m (63,800ft), limited by the mechanical time fuze to

Indian Army gunners operating a Bofors gun in Italy, 1944. Notice above the loader's head a hand is adjusting the sights.

A special lightweight version of the Bofors gun was developed for use by airborne troops and for towing behind a jeep.

13,700m (45,000ft). Although only intended as a stop-gap, the Mk 6 gun performed so well that it remained in service for the remainder of heavy anti-aircraft gunnery days, not being declared obsolete until 1959.

The 'Intermediate AA Gun' was a much more difficult proposition and one which never did become successful. Two solutions were offered: a 3-pounder, then under development for the Navy, and a 57mm 6-pounder which had been designed before the war by Bofors, and which was more or less an enlargement of the 40mm gun. The 3-pounder was turned down because the shell was not thought to be large enough, while the Bofors design was only available on a naval pattern of twin-gun mounting.

In January 1941, it was decided to develop a new 6-pounder gun, and a specification was issued calling for a weapon giving a ceiling of 3,000m (10,000ft), a time of flight to that height of five seconds, and automatic fire at 100 rounds per minute. By the end of that year, a two-barrelled equipment on a three-wheeled carriage had been designed, and a pilot model was built during 1942. In December 1942, the Director General of Artillery asked for a single-gun model to be developed, using an automatic loader that the Molins Company had developed for use with the 6-pounder tank gun. The first designs for this were submitted in April 1943, but they were considered unsuitable for various reasons, and the work began again. Fresh designs were submitted in December 1943 and it was then decided to build six pilot models, three fitted with electric remote power control, and three with hydraulic RPC, both achieving a traverse speed of 25 degrees per second.

In February 1944, a new complication was added by a General Staff decision that the weapons had to be suitable for the dual role of AA guns and anti-motor-torpedo-boat (AMTB) guns, and this was further confused by a decision in June 1944 to modify the existing twin 6-pounder coast defence AMTB guns to allow them to fire in the AA role.

The next problem arose in October 1944, when the Director Royal Artillery, pointing to the increased speed of jet aircraft, demanded that the equipment be capable of accurate fire against 965km/h (600mph) targets at 400m (1,300ft) range; this meant a gun capable of traversing at 45 degrees per second and it put the existing designs clean out of the running. In December 1944, it was decided to build twelve prototype single-gun equipments utilizing various RPC systems and different designs of carriage in the hope of hitting on a combination that would provide a solution.

To recapitulate this tangled story: by

A 3.7-inch Mark 6 gun at maximum elevation.

December 1944, two twin-gun equipments had been built, one with automatic loading and one without; a dozen single-gun prototypes had been authorized; the twin equipments were being re-designed in order to give them an AMTB capability; and, in the reverse direction, the existing 6-pounder AMTB equipment was being re-designed to give it an AA capability. None of the weapons so far built had been satisfactory from the ballistic point of view or from the standpoint of mechanical reliability; they were extremely cumbersome and could not deliver the volume of fire demanded, probably because the whole project relied on developing a high-speed loading system for a gun that, originally, had been designed for hand loading. The mechanical loading gear on the twin mounting was a staggering piece of complexity that rarely managed to perform for any length of time without breaking down.

Finally, on 30 March 1945, the War Office decided that: 'Owing to the difficulties in obtaining satisfactory reliability with the 6-pounder AA Twin equipment, and since the designed performance is out of date with modern high-speed aircraft targets, together with the planned development of a fully automatic single 6-pounder equipment, the twin equipment will not be introduced into Land Service.' Development of the single gun continued for some time after the war but, with the rapid development of jet aircraft, the 1941 Specification became even more out of date and the project was finally abandoned as a potential gun, although work on the automatic loading gear did continue, since this yielded considerable amounts of fundamental research information for a post-war project on high-speed loading systems known as 'Project Ratefixer'. But, as the German Army had also found out, the Intermediate AA Gun was an extremely difficult proposition, which had been solved by neither country during the war years, and which, perhaps fortunately, was eventually to be resolved by the guided missile.

The 6-pounder AA gun was properly known as the 6-pounder 6cwt in order to distinguish it from the anti-tank 6-pounder 7cwt, and the

The pilot model of the twin 6-pounder intermediate AA gun. From this angle the complexities of the automatic loading gear are, mercifully, concealed.

The twin 6-pounder in travelling mode.

coast defence 6-pounder 10cwt. It was broadly based on the 6-pounder 7cwt, but was larger and had a larger chamber taking a bigger cartridge case. The carriages were three-wheeled, with removable axles, the two front wheels having Ackermann steering. Four outriggers could be lowered and hydraulic jacks could be used to level the mounting after the wheels had been removed. Remote Power Control gear was fitted in addition to hand-operated elevating and traverse gears, and a hand-fed hopper behind the guns held eight rounds. The automatic loading gear was behind the gun and was driven by the recoil force.

The zenith of British air-defence gunnery came in the late summer of 1944 with the launching of the German V-1 pilotless flying bomb. By that time some more technological links had been added to the defensive chain, notably the American SCR584 radar set and its associated Bell computer, and the proximity fuze.

The SCR584 was a centimetric radar with a detection range in excess of 70,000 yards (64km) and the ability to lock on and track a target without human intervention, delivering a

constant stream of data to the predictor. The predictor was fully electronic and could deal with data far faster than previous models; it could cope with targets up to 965km/h (600mph) and it delivered gun data with sufficient power to directly operate a remote power-controlled gun. All the gunners had to do was keep loading it; aiming and firing was all performed by the predictor.

The third technical innovation to appear at the eleventh hour was the electronic proximity fuze. As far back as 1938, when the radar scientists were first confronted with gunnery, the errors inherent in calculating and setting fuzes had drawn their attention. An early suggestion was to make a fuze which carried a simple receiver and thus pick up the radar signals reflected from the target by the early-warning set or gun-laying set, and thus cause the shell to detonate when it got close enough, but the signal strengths involved were far too weak for this idea to be made to work at that period of radar's development. Later came the proposal to put a complete radio transmitter/receiver unit into the fuze so that it would emit its own signal and, when close to the target, would *proximity*

detect the echo of this signal and detonate the ~~fuse~~ shell. This promised better results and much of the theoretical work was done in 1939–40, but the possibility of having such devices made in Britain was practically zero at that time. So in 1940 the proximity fuze was one of the many things taken to the USA by the Tizard Mission. The United States Navy were attracted by the idea and undertook the development; the Eastman Kodak Company became the prime contractors, with the various components being made by such specialists as Sylvania, Westinghouse, Emerson, Philco, General Electric, Exide and other well-known names in the radio and electrical field. After satisfying the Navy's demands, designs were worked out for Army AA guns and later for ground-fire applications, and in mid-1944 the first Fuze, VT, T98 for the 3.7-inch AA gun were coming from the production line. (The letters 'VT', used to identify this type of fuze for many years, are often said to mean 'variable time', a fiction that was tacitly encouraged. In fact the fuzes were not time fuzes, nor were they variable; the letters came about because the development was begun by Section 'V' of the US Navy Bureau of Ordnance and it happened to be that Bureau's 'Project T'.)

The story of the flying bomb and the rest of the German V-weapons has been often enough told and there is no space to go into great detail here. The prime facts are that, due to good intelligence and astute reasoning, the AA Command were prepared well in advance, even though they were not entirely sure of what they were going to have to deal with. The outline plans for 'Operation Diver', as the anti-flying bomb campaign was known, were draw up in December 1943 with plans to move 500 heavy and 800 light guns into place to protect London, Bristol and Southampton. A thicket of balloons would be planted around the south-eastern edge of London, a line of guns across the North Downs from Redhill to the Isle of Sheppey, and the RAF fighters would deal with everything in front of the gun belt. Unfortunately this plan had to be scrapped almost as soon as it was made when it became apparent that (a) the flying bombs were not about to appear as soon as expected, and (b) several of the regiments earmarked for 'Diver' were also earmarked for the invasion of Europe, and the latter had priority. A fresh plan, 'Overlord Diver', was drawn up, reducing the number of guns to be deployed. In fact it reduced the number so severely that on D-Day (6 June 1944) London would be left with only fifty-four guns.

The V-1 attack commenced, on schedule, on 13 June 1944, but this was simply a gesture by the German field commander; his orders were to fire the first bombs on that date, and by superhuman efforts on the part of his men, he did. But he then closed down for a couple of days to get his organization running properly and all his equipment in working order before resuming that attack on 15 June.

AA Command spent the two-day period of grace in organizing the defences, bringing in 192 light and 192 heavy guns in a matter of four days, and by 28 June there were 376 heavy and 576 light guns deployed across the North Downs, plus another 520 20mm and 40mm guns manned by the RAF Regiment, which were usually used as airfield protection. A further 441 static 3.7-inch guns were in process of being uprooted from their sites all over England and carted down to Kent on tank transporters when Air Marshal Sir Roderick Hill, in overall command of the Diver operation, and General Pile, AA Commander-in-Chief, got together and decided on a change of tactics.

A member of Hill's staff had done a very careful study of the battle so far and reached the conclusion that the aircraft and the guns should change places. If the guns were along the coast, they could have an unrestricted field of fire; behind them the fighters could have the sky to themselves, and a second group of fighters could be well out to sea, beyond the range of the guns, to act as the first line of defence. What they missed the guns would attack, with no restrictions on firing, and what they missed the second group of fighters would mop up. Bearing in mind that some of the guns had only just got into place and that some 400 more were actually moving at the time, the decision to make such a sweeping change was not an easy one, but it was taken and, in the face of a great deal of opposition by the Air Staff, it was carried out. A total of 23,000 men and women, 800 guns and 60,000 tons of ammunition and stores had to be lifted and moved.

By 19 July the new 'Diver Belt' was in action, but almost immediately it was seen that the Germans had moved their operation north and were outflanking the Diver Belt by flying the bombs up the Thames Estuary: an extension, the 'Diver Box' was added in north Kent.

Eventually there were 800 heavy guns, 1,800 light guns, and 700 rocket launchers deployed, with another 144 heavy guns in reserve.

It was at this point that General Pile approached General Marshall, the US Chief of Staff and asked for SCR584 radars, predictors and proximity fuzes. Marshall agreed and 165 SCR 584s were shipped immediately, together with several thousand fuzes; they arrived in Britain at the end of June and were immediately sent down to the Diver Belt to be put into use. For a few days chaos reigned as gun positions had two sets of equipment, with the gunners learning all about SCR 584 in between bouts of shooting at bombs with GL3. Once they became familiar with the new material, the old was withdrawn.

As the Allied invasion force worked its way northwards from the landing beachhead of Normandy, so the German V-1 launching teams

A Bofors gun troop in the Diver Belt goes into action.

The ultimate in World War Two AA radar was this Radar No 4 Mark 7, which provided the early warning element and also, by means of the separate antenna seen here, distinguished between friend and foe.

Things get bigger all the time. The 5.25-inch AA gun before installation into its gun-house, showing some of the mass of hydraulic equipment which elevated, traversed and loaded the gun.

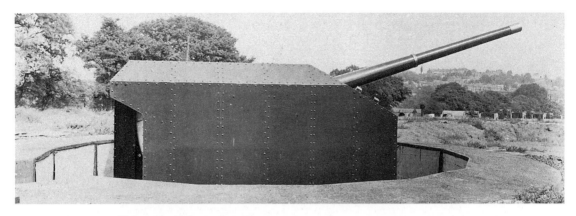

A 5.25-inch gun installed on the outskirts of London.

This shows that there was more to a 5.25-inch installation than met the eye; quite a large proportion of the mounting was below ground level, and below that were the magazine and engine room which provided the hydraulic power.

moved ahead, thus altering their line of attack. And as the bombs arrived further north, so the southern end of the Diver Strip was uprooted and rushed up to extend the line northwards, until the greater part of the defensive strip was in East Anglia. The end finally came when the last bomb was blown out of the sky on 28 March 1945 by a 3.7-inch gun at Orfordness.

In all, some 10,492 V-1 bombs were launched against Britain; of these, 3,213 failed to reach Britain due to mechanical or other defects; 1,847 were destroyed by RAF fighters, 1,878 by AA guns and twenty-three by colliding with barrage balloons. A total of 3,531 succeeded in getting past the defences, of which 2,419 reached the London Civil Defence area. These overall figures are somewhat deceptive, since they are skewed by the tactical change halfway through the campaign. In the final phase, in which 275 missiles were launched and 125 reached Britain, the guns got eighty-seven, fighters four, and only thirteen got past the defences.

A less well-known V-1 assault was made against Antwerp between October 1944 and February 1945. In this battle no aircraft or balloons were involved, the entire defence of the area being accomplished by artillery, both British and American. Altogether 4,883 bombs

A battery of 5.25-inch guns preserved at Princess Alexandra's Battery, Gibraltar. These were sited so as to function as both air defence and coast defence guns.

were launched against Antwerp; of these only 211 landed within 8 miles of the centre of Antwerp docks. Of the 211, fifty-five had got past the defences when the guns had been silenced to permit Allied bombers to fly through the area; the remaining 156 were fired on but not hit. From a kill rate of 67 per cent at the start of the campaign, it improved to 97 per cent at the end.

The final wartime development in British AA artillery, and the most powerful AA gun to see service, was the British 5.25-inch; it will be recalled that this was offered as the long-term solution to the heavy-gun question, the 3.7-inch Mark 6 being merely a stopgap. But converting a shipboard dual-purpose gun into a land-based anti-aircraft gun took some time. A completely new power-driven mounting had to be developed, together with emplacements, engine rooms and a new family of ammunition. The resulting weapon could send its 36.3kg (80lb) shell to a maximum ceiling of 17,000m (56,000ft), and the detonation of such a shell made a very impressive lethal area. Installation around London and various naval bases and dockyards began in late 1944 and continued into the early 1950s at a cost said at the time to be half a million pounds per gun. Most of the guns were sited so as to be capable of acting as either coast defence or anti-aircraft weapons as the situation demanded. But the programme was slowed down and finally cancelled with the closure of coast defence and the arrival of guided missiles in the mid-1950s.

GERMANY

By 1941 the RAF had built up sufficient strength to begin bombing Germany and the German defences had begun to demonstrate their efficiency. This defence rested primarily on the 88mm and 105mm guns, several hundred batteries of which were distributed across Germany. Their information came largely from ground observers and sound location, with early warning provided by a handful of Freya radar sets. In addition there were several-hundred searchlight batteries, each equipped with three lights and a sound locator. The full strength in September 1940 was impressive: 2,870 heavy guns, 7,970 light and medium guns, 2,540 searchlights and 380 balloons; and these figures did not include naval weapons emplaced on shore around dockyards and naval bases.

So far as technical development went, it was largely concerned with extracting the utmost performance from existing guns by improving ammunition. Controlled fragmentation of shells – to ensure that the pieces were large enough to do significant damage to an aircraft – was exhaustively studied and several experimental designs tested; reduction of drag by better shaping was another path of research, as was the adaptation of the fin-stabilized 'dart shell' – originally designed for long-range firing with heavy artillery – to the anti-aircraft role so as to achieve higher velocity and shorter times of flight.

The only major gun improvement was the upgrading of the 88mm Flak design. A specification had been issued in the autumn of 1939 – Rheinmetall-Borsig being given the contract – and their first prototype was ready for trial in early 1941; it was a very good design indeed. Instead of the Flak 18's pedestal the gun was mounted on a turntable and trunnioned close to the breech, to be as low-set as possible. The ballistics were greatly improved, and a roller loading-mechanism drawing its power from a hydro-pneumatic piston operated on recoil speeded up the rate of fire. The most adventurous part of the design was the barrel, but here, in the opinion of many authorities, Rheinmetall's designers overreached themselves. Like the Flak 18, the barrel was divided into three bore sections with a sleeve, a jacket and a locking collar to hold everything together. But the new Flak 41 had a much higher chamber pressure, and the steel car-

The German 88mm Flak 41 was a low-set, turntable-mounted gun rarely seen outside Germany . . .

tridge-case necks expanded into the joints between the sections and then failed to contract, so that the case stuck in the chamber instead of extracting.

Special brass cases were developed, which overcame the trouble to some degree, but it periodically re-occurred, and the design was eventually changed to a two-section liner with jacket and sleeve. The 152 guns issued with the original three-piece liner were marked with a yellow band around the barrel indicating that they were only to be used with ammunition having brass cartridge cases. A further 133 guns were then issued with two-piece barrels, but the trouble persisted, though to a smaller degree. The design was again changed to a heavier two-piece barrel with a jacket and no sleeve, and the remainder of production (some 271 guns) used this third type of barrel. In spite of all this

trouble the Flak 41 was a good weapon, and a number were used by the Czechoslovakian army until the early 1960s.

The German air defence organization was headed by a *Flugwachkommando* (Air Watch Command), a form of control centre which received warning information from the Freya radars forming part of the *Flugmeldestellen* (Air Reporting Posts), and also from a network of ground observer posts. In the *Wachkommando,* information was assessed and the appropriate *Flakgruppen* covering districts likely to be the target of an oncoming raid were warned. These, in turn, passed the information to the *Flakuntergruppe* that had direct command of the flak batteries, and the guns would receive a preliminary warning when a raid entered a circle of 200km radius around the gun site.

. . . an exception being this one, captured in Tunisia in 1943.

The Freya radar had a range of about 160km (100 miles) and was a good early-warning detector but too imprecise for the direction of guns. It was, in fact, a German naval set; the Luftwaffe's radar development programme had fallen behind and, after a bitter wrangle, a few Freyas were handed over to the Luftwaffe early in 1940. The Luftwaffe's own design, developed by the Telefunken Company, eventually came into service as the Würzburg. The prototype had been demonstrated to Hitler in February 1939 and went into production in April 1940, but like most innovative devices it took some time to make the production models perform properly and to train people to extract the best from them. Shortly before production got under way an experimental model was developed, with a greatly improved method of measuring target height, and once this had been perfected production of the first model (Würzburg A) was stopped after some 200 had been made and its place was taken by the new Würzburg C, of which 1,000 were eventually made and installed. Würzburg was a far more advanced and precise instrument than Freya

and could direct gunfire quite accurately, but it was to be the middle of 1941 before it came into widespread use.

In the absence of radar the Luftwaffe had placed a great deal of faith in infra-red radiation as a means of detecting targets, and a number of devices made an appearance. At least a dozen, bearing names such as 'Popeye', 'Frogs-eye', 'Buttercup' and 'Wunsdorf' were designed for installation in fighter aircraft so as to detect the hot exhausts of the Allied bomber engines. Most of these were abandoned in 1942 when radar development had reached the point of airborne equipment, but one device, known as 'Kiel' and made by Zeiss, was still in production when the war ended. This used a lead sulphide detection-cell mounted in the focus of a parabolic mirror in the nose of the aircraft (usually a Messerschmitt 110) and was claimed to be able to detect targets up to 5km away.

Adlergerät, Kormoran, Mucke, Obt and Walter were all varieties of infra-red telescope for use by AA guns and searchlights, enabling exhausts to be picked up visually in darkness and thus providing data for insertion into a pre-

But the 88 Flak 18/36 was seen everywhere; and frequently, as is this one, employed in the field or anti-tank role.

dictor or for aligning a searchlight before switching it on, ensuring rapid acquisition of the target and less chance of evasive action by the aircraft. Most of these equipments failed to come up to expectations, though the Adlergerät was in fairly wide use in 1940 and 1941 before the Würzburg radars appeared.

The original disposition of German defences was much as might be expected; cities and towns were ringed with searchlights and guns, while fighter aircraft were dispersed at a number of bases. On being alerted by a radar intercept, the fighters would take to the air to fly standing patrols within range of a radio beacon, which would give them further instructions. Unfortunately, while patrolling, the fighters frequently came into the searchlight zones and were promptly shot at by their own gunners. Another drawback was that the rings of lights defined the target areas and gave the RAF bombers an excellent form of guidance. To cure these defects Colonel Josef Kammhuber, head of night-fighting defences, redeployed the lights and many of the guns into a line stretching from Denmark to Belgium, thus placing the defensive zone well out from the major industrial areas. Fighters were to be guided to their targets by ground controllers,

who based their instructions on indications from the Freya radar, but due to the poor accuracy of this set successful interceptions were few and what damage the RAF sustained was principally from gunfire.

The Germans, like the British, realized that they had a more or less undefended layer of sky between about 3,000 and 5,000m (10,000 to 16,500ft), too high for their 37mm gun and too low for their 88mm and larger weapons. Indeed, it appears that they were the first to spot the problem and, as early as 1935, Rheinmetall were given a contract to develop a 5cm gun, which entered service as the 5cm Flak 41 in November 1940. It was a gas-operated automatic gun using a vertical sliding breechblock and feeding from the left side. The mounting was a triangular platform with two 2-wheeled axles and two folding outriggers. It was dropped into action and roughly levelled by jacks on the outriggers, then accurately levelled by screws in the base ring of the gun pedestal, a system that added unnecessary weight and complication. Less than 200 guns were built. Although it fired a 4.3kg (9.5lb) shell to 5,600m (18,000ft) ceiling at 130 rounds per minute, the *Luftwaffe* considered it a failure. It was unstable both when firing and travelling due to a high centre of gravity, it

Loading the 88mm Flak 18/36. The man on the left is operating the fuze setter, while the man on the right is waiting to drop the next round in after the loader has removed the round currently being set.

was difficult to conceal, it could not track targets fast enough, and the complex optical calculating sight was poor at arithmetic and far too complicated. Nevertheless, it was kept in service; it had been a useful test-bed for the 'intermediate AA gun theory' and had demonstrated that such a gun, if it worked well, was a desirable property.

After the 5cm Flak 41 had been abandoned, the Luftwaffe sat down and thoroughly examined the intermediate gun concept, and they came to the conclusion that development of such a gun was only justified in defensive areas where it was vital to destroy 100 per cent of the attacking aircraft, situations where even a single aircraft getting through could cause a disaster – such as the raid on the Möhne Dam. If a gun guaranteed this 100 per cent success, no price was too high to pay for it, and the solution deduced was to employ a six-gun battery remotely controlled from a predictor.

What evolved from this was what would today be called a 'weapons system', in which the radar, the predictor, the displacement corrector and the guns were all tailored to each other and

formed a cohesive package. The gun was to be of 5.5cm calibre, a choice conditioned partly by the Flak 41's shortcomings and the tactical concept outlined above, and partly by Rheinmetall-Borsig's discovery early in 1942 that the 5cm calibre was ballistically unsuitable: it was impossible to produce a shell of the required destructive power that would also be stable at the high velocities demanded. The destructive power was based on a ruling that the explosive content was to be 500g (17.6oz), which had been proved by experiment to be the minimum amount necessary to guarantee the destruction of a heavy bomber with one shot. The velocity demanded was high, to reduce the time of flight and thus improve both the accuracy and the chance of hitting. Rheinmetall proposed the 5.5cm calibre and, after considerable delay while the whole 'medium anti-aircraft problem' was evaluated, the Luftwaffe finally agreed and issued the specification. Perfecting the ammunition and designing the various other components of the system took up most of 1943. By the spring of 1944 prototype ammunition and guns had been fired and

The 5cm Flak 41 was a first try for an intermediate AA gun, but it wasn't quite good enough.

Another view of the 5cm Flak 41 in the firing position.

This is believed to be the second prototype 5.5cm Flak, there being some small differences in the carriage.

One of Germany's first SPAA guns was this 2cm Flak mounted on a Demag 7 semi-tracked carrier, adopted in 1937.

the results gave rise to a good deal of rethinking. Several different designs of shell were then tried in turn, together with various twists of rifling, but the question of what was finally to be the service standard was never settled before the war ended.

The gun itself was little more than an enlarged version of the 5cm Flak 41, using the same basic mechanism. But in order to improve stability when firing, the gun was equipped with the same sort of differential recoil system that Krupp had applied to their 5cm gun in 1909. The gun fired, and was reloaded during the recoil and run-out strokes, firing before it had completely run out. Thus the explosion and the subsequent recoil thrust had first to overcome the inertia of the forward-moving mass before starting it on its recoil stroke again; the net result was a considerable reduction in the recoil stress placed on the mounting.

The mounting was also an enlargement of the two-axle Flak 41 design, but it was also intended to develop static and self-propelled mountings in due course, in addition to a twin-gun version. A notable feature of both the gun and the mounting design was the extensive use of stamped sheet-metal components in order to simplify production. In early 1945 a project was begun to attach a squeeze-bore muzzle unit to the gun in order to get even more velocity out of it.

The long delay in the ammunition development, together with the late start of the project and its ambitious ancillaries, was unfortunate. Although three prototype guns were built, the remainder of the programme never reached the production stage before the war ended. It is generally accepted that the Soviet 57mm anti-aircraft gun of 1950 represents the final results of the work begun by Rheinmetall-Borsig in 1943.

THE USA

Throughout the early 1920s the 4.7-inch AA gun demanded by General Pershing in 1918 kept coming back like a boomerang, but by 1926 the Ordnance Department had reluctantly decided that it was far too cumbersome and complicated, given the current technology, and that it should be shelved in favour of more practical things like the 3-inch and 105mm guns, to be resuscitated as and when the technology appeared to favour the project.

In 1938 the time was judged to be ripe and the project for a 4.7-inch gun was revived; military characteristics were specified, the matter was debated, and on 1 June 1939 authority was given for design work to start. One gets the feeling that a fair amount of work must have been going on in spare moments since 1926,

The prototype of the 5.5cm Flak gun.

because the design was completed and the 4.7-inch Gun M1 (later redesignated 120mm Gun M1) formally introduced in late 1940 and, to anybody looking at the weapon with a critical eye, it is obvious that a design of this complexity was not completed from scratch in eighteen months. The gun was a conventional design, sixty-calibres long and with a semi-automatic vertical sliding-block breech mechanism. The mounting was also conventional, if massive, with a central platform upon which the top carriage and gun revolved, stabilized by four folding outriggers. The mounting was carried on two axles, each with two double wheels, which were removed when the gun was brought into action.

The complications set in with the arrangements for fuze-setting and ramming. The gun fired a 50lb (22.6kg) shell; the brass cartridge case was 33in (84cm) long and 7.5in (19cm) across the base, and contained 23.6lb (10.7kg) of powder. The complete round weighed 98lb 6oz (44.6kg) and it was obvious that, in the first

place, nobody could be expected to lift and then throw it into the breech by hand and, in the second place, it was impossible to make it as a fixed, one-piece round. It had to be loaded in two moves, first the shell and then the cartridge.

By this time, mechanical ramming of a fixed round was a practical matter, but mechanical ramming of a separate-loading round had never been tried. Moreover, somewhere in the business of mechanically loading the two components, the time fuze had to be set and a constant dead time introduced into the operation. The solution was a brilliant piece of engineering and one of the factors that makes me suspicious of the eighteen-month development time.

Behind the breech was a loading tray, the rear section of which curved upwards. Above this was a rammer mechanism that terminated in a swinging arm, the tip of which followed the curved section of the loading tray. Above the breech ring of the gun, carried on the cradle, was the fuze setter. The loading tray and

The US 120mm M1 gun in its final form.

Side view of the 120mm M1 showing the folded outriggers. The box on top of the gun is the casing inside which the fuze-setting machine fitted.

Another view of the 120mm M1 shows how the gun was retracted into the fully recoiled position for travelling, so as not to place excessive strain on the elevating gears.

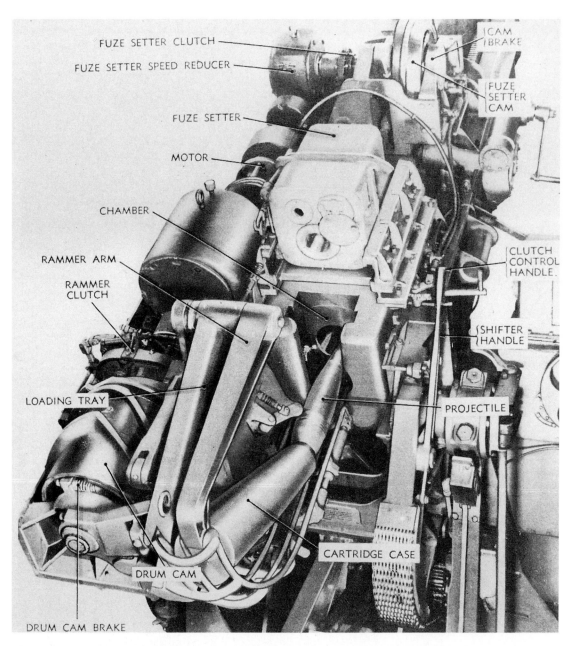

FUZE SETTER CLUTCH
FUZE SETTER SPEED REDUCER
FUZE SETTER
MOTOR
CHAMBER
RAMMER ARM
RAMMER CLUTCH
LOADING TRAY
DRUM CAM BRAKE
DRUM CAM
CAM BRAKE
FUZE SETTER CAM
CLUTCH CONTROL HANDLE.
SHIFTER HANDLE
PROJECTILE
CARTRIDGE CASE

The ramming mechanism of the 120mm M1 gun, with a shell and cartridge in position ready to be rammed.

rammer were carried on a pivoted shaft lying parallel to the gun's axis.

One man carried a shell to the gun and dumped it on to the straight front portion of the loading tray. A second man carried the cartridge, the mouth of which was closed by a thick and resilient cork plug; he dropped this into the loading tray so that the cork plug was at the base of the shell and the rear end was well up the curved section of the loading tray. Having dropped the cartridge case into place, he stepped back and punched a button.

The whole unit – rammer, rammer arm, loading tray, cartridge and shell – was now swung up, revolving on the pivoted shaft, so that the nose of the shell came opposite the fuze setter. The rammer arm moved down far enough to press the cartridge case firmly into contact with the shell, thus supporting the shell, while the fuze setter slide backwards to surround the fuze and set it. The fuze setter then ran forward into its rest position and the loading unit now swung down, around the pivoted shaft, until the nose of the shell was opposite the open breech. The rammer arm was now propelled at considerable speed, swinging

in an arc and giving the cartridge case an uppercut that drove it and the shell straight into the chamber. The shell clanged into the rifling, the rim of the cartridge case pressed the extractors forward, releasing the breechblock to slide up and close, while the rammer unit swung upwards and out of the path of recoil as the gun fired. The gun recoiled, the breech opened on the run-out stroke and the cartridge case was ejected and, as the gun returned to battery, so the rammer dropped down ready for the next round. With a well-drilled (and muscular) detachment a rate of twelve rounds per minute could be maintained.

A total of 550 of these equipments were built, but with a travelling weight of 61,500lbs (27.45 tons) they were not considered suitable for service with field armies, and apart from four guns sent to Northern Ireland (probably in error) and a handful sent to the Panama Canal Zone to replace the 105mm guns, none ever left the continental United States. It is perhaps worth remarking that in later years this gun formed the starting point for the development of the massive M59 120mm tank gun, which was adopted by both the US (M103 heavy tank)

About to fire a 120mm M1 gun; the loader has just placed the cartridge in position and moved the rammer arm into contact with the cartridge base.

and UK (Conqueror heavy tank) armies during the late 1950s.

As 1941 came into its final month, the Japanese attack on Pearl Harbor (detected by radar but ignored) brought the United States into the war and, as had happened elsewhere, brought the air defences into the limelight. While the prospect of an enemy flying as far as the USA had always been discounted, the Pearl Harbor demonstration of the potential of carrier-borne aircraft put a new complexion on the aerial threat and heightened it by having destroyed much of the naval shield intended to protect the Pacific coast from attack.

During 1939 the first early radar (known then as 'Derax') sets, the SCR270 (mobile) and SCR271 (static) were perfected and production begun, and in 1940 the first operational sets were installed in the Panama Canal Zone. The SCR268 gun control set had also been built and demonstrated, but lack of funds and personnel had reduced progress to little more than a token effort. It was not until the Tizard mission went from Britain to the USA in August 1940 to reveal British radar progress and, in particular, the resonant cavity magnetron, the device which enabled high power to be developed on extremely short (centimetric) wave-lengths, that radar research in the USA really gathered speed.

The replacement for the 3-inch guns, the 90mm Gun M1, entered service at the proverbial eleventh hour, just prior to the war striking the USA but too late for any guns to be in place when the attack came, and the action in the Philippines was conducted by the 3-inch static guns mounted in the harbour defences of Manila and Subic Bay plus a handful of mobile guns. In 1940 there were no less than 807 3-inch AA guns of various types on the US Army's inventory, but apart from those deployed in the Philippine Islands and other Pacific dependencies, they were fated to spend their war as training guns.

As with Britain and Germany, so, more or

SATURDAY, AUGUST 3, 1935

ARMY'S MYSTERY RAY

SENSATIONAL NEW DEVICE TO SEE IN DARK

By
Copyright, 1935, by Universal Service.
PORT MONMOUTH, N. J., Aug. 2.—The inside story of the United States Army's new so-called "mystery ray," which is expected to revolutionize warfare, was told exclusively to this writer for the first time by a "high" Army official today.

The apparatus, which has been successfully tested during the last few nights in mimic warfare to guard the entrance to New York Harbor, receives a "mystery ray," instead of projecting it, as first reported.

By use of the sensational device, which utilizes the most modern principles of television and the "infra-red ray," invisible enemy battle fleets and airplane squadrons can be seen in full detail, despite darkness.

PICTURE OF ENEMY

A picture of the attacking fleet or ships or planes actually appears on a small screen, in a kind of midget "movie," and its location is automatically charted. The receiving device gathers up the invisible "infra-red rays" and brings them, through a television "scanning" apparatus, to the screen. When the receiver is properly focused the image of the ship appears as clearly as in daylight.

It was found that the infra-red ray, which lies just beyond the edge of the light spectrum visible to the human eye, could be detected by an apparatus similar to that of the ultra-short-wave receivers designed by the Italian inventor Marconi.

RAYS CAN'T BE SEEN

The infra-red ray, otherwise known as the "heat ray," is produced without exception by all heated objects, from red-hot coal to a warm hot-water bottle. The rays have never been "seen," but their presence can be detected in two ways—by the sense of feeling —which shows them as heat—and by the newly-perfected receptor.

The rays are given off by the engine of a battleship, or that of an airplane, so long as there is any heat whatsoever remaining in the metal. And the rays, like the rays of light, illuminate surrounding objects.

As a result of this discovery, by "grafting" a "heat-ray" detecting apparatus on a television apparatus, the signal corps was able to "see," on a silver screen, a heated object in a dark room. After this, an airplane motor was brought in, run for a while, and then, in utter darkness, "seen" in the laboratory.

An American newspaper of 1935 gets the scoop on the 'invisible ray which will revolutionize warfare'.

less with the USA: they finished the war with the same guns that they had at the start, having upgraded their principal gun halfway through. The 90mm Gun M1 was approved for production on 21 March 1940. The gun used a monobloc tube sliding in guide rails and fitted with a semi-automatic vertical sliding breech-block. The M1 mounting was a four-outrigger platform of unusual design, since it used a single axle with two dual wheels. One outrigger was fixed to act as a towing-bar, while the other three folded up for travelling. The top carriage

What the 'invisible ray' actually turned out to be was this SCR268 gun control radar.

An American 90mm M1 gun in Alaska.

was fitted with hand-operated elevation and traverse gears, and with data dials for the reception of electrically-transmitted data from the director.

On 22 May 1941, the Mount M1A1 was standardized, together with the Gun M1A1. The mount was much the same as before, except that it now had provision for remote power control, and the cradle was fitted with the Spring Rammer M8. This was a cylinder, above the gun barrel, which contained springs and a ramming rod; as the gun recoiled the spring was compressed and the ramming rod extended. As the cartridge entered the breech ring, pulling a trip lever released the spring-loaded rod and rammed the round into the breech. In fact, the Spring Rammer M8 turned out to be more trouble than it was worth and it was invariably disconnected or removed by the gunners.

Although formally approved in 1941, the M1A1 equipment actually went into production late in 1940, in advance of approval and on high priority; by the time of the North African

Setting the fuze prior to loading a 90mm gun in the Pacific theatre, apparently doing some ground firing.

landings in 1942, more than 2,000 equipments had been made and issued. It became the standard field army AA gun and was used in every theatre of war.

At the time of the introduction of the M1A1, the Coast Artillery requested a static mount capable of being used as an anti-torpedo-boat gun in harbour defences as a secondary role. As a result, the M3 mounting was developed, a straight-forward pedestal mount fitted with a shield. Although there were minor differences, these mounts were virtually the top carriage assembly of the mobile mount M1A1 bolted down to a holdfast in concrete.

While the M1A1 equipment was satisfactory from the pure-AA point of view, the Chiefs of Staff decided that what was needed was an equipment capable of more rapid response in an emergency – the M1A1 took some time to get into action – capable of engaging ground

targets and capable of functioning as a mobile coast-defence gun. Even if the M1A1 could have been got into action more rapidly, it was incapable of depressing below point blank, which ruled it out as a coast-defence weapon. On 11 September 1942, the new project was begun, and on 13 May 1943, the Gun M2 on Mount M2 was standardized.

The M2 gun was much the same as the M1, except for the method of attachment of the breech ring – interrupted threads instead of a continuous one. But the Mount M2 was a considerable change; it was now a two-axle cruciform mount with outriggers, folding shields and folding platforms. It was provided with hand or remote power control of elevation and traverse. The cradle incorporated the Fuze Setter and Rammer M20, driven by an electric motor above the gun; this was a roller ramming-system, very similar to that used with the

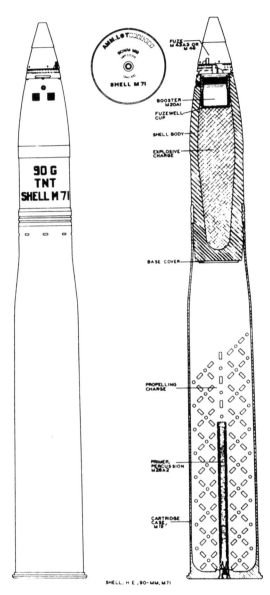

A complete round of ammunition for the US 90mm gun. The shell was about the same size as that of the British 25-pounder field gun.

German 105mm Flak 38. The principal difference was that the round was not placed on a loading tray, but simply thrust into the open breech between two rollers that were rotating at low speed and that drew the round forward.

Between the rollers and the mouth of the gun chamber was a casing containing a set of jaws not unlike a drill chuck; as the round was drawn forward and the fuze entered this casing, the ramming rollers stopped and the jaws contracted to set the fuze. The jaws then opened sufficiently to clear the cartridge case, the ramming rollers accelerated to high speed, and the round was propelled into the gun breech; as the cartridge rim struck the extractors this released the breechblock, which slammed shut, and the gun fired.

As the round left the rollers they retracted into the breech ring and, when the gun fired, the empty cartridge case ejected through the fuze-setter casing, and past the rollers, which then moved in again and began rotating, ready to accept the next round. For firing proximity or percussion fuzes, the fuze-setting function could be locked out of operation and the ramming rollers then rotated at high speed all the time, to load the cartridge without interruption. Like many such devices, it sounds a lot more complicated than it really was and it certainly gave very little trouble in service, while it put the rate of fire up from fifteen to twenty-seven rounds per minute. At the minimum fuze setting, the whole process of loading took 2.6 seconds.

In 1940, with war clouds on the horizon, the US Navy's interest in the Bofors gun was revived, because by that time they had discovered that the Hudson was satisfactory provided you had a meticulously trained crew, but that hastily trained conscript sailors were incapable of keeping it in action. It was then suggested that the US Army might care to look at the Bofors as well, so as to achieve some standardization across the board. In late 1940 both the US Navy and the Army acquired sample guns from Britain and, after trials and examination of the weapons, the Army's wheeled gun was standardized as the Gun M1 on Carriage M1 in May 1941 and negotiations were opened with Bofors to obtain a licence to manufacture.

The 90mm M2 gun was a much more advanced design, with full remote power-control on tap, plus a mechanical ramming system which owed something to the German 105mm design.

Apart from the fact that this has single wheels instead of double, it is all too easy to confuse the 90mm M2 with the 120mm M1 when packed for travelling.

FUNCTIONING OF FUZE SETTER-RAMMER

1. Breech open, ramming rolls closed and rotating at low speed—fuze jaws closed.

2. Round stationary, ramming rolls stalled and fuze jaws rotating fuze ring.

3. Round jammed by ramming rolls rotating at high speed—fuze jaws open.

4. Breech closed, gun is fired—in recoil ramming rolls open.

5. Breech opened in counterrecoil, cartridge case ejected. Gun moves into battery, ramming rolls close and rotate at low speed—fuze jaws close.

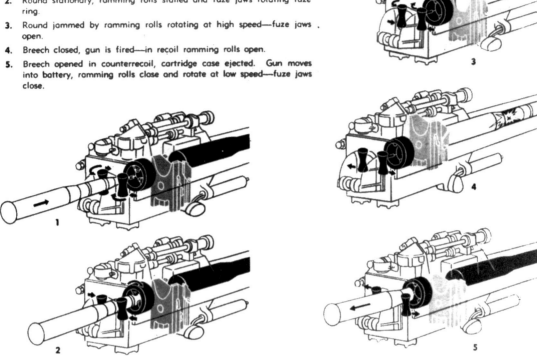

A handbook drawing showing the operation of the fuze setter/rammer on the 90mm Gun M2.

The equipment that the Army had obtained from Britain was an original Swedish-made Bofors, and there were some features of the carriage that did not sit well with American manufacturing methods. The Firestone company was given a contract to re-design it to conform with US standards, with the result that it acquired a welded frame, tubular axles, a simplified pivot, the inevitable Warner electric brakes, and several other minor details. The resulting design was standardized in December 1941 as the Carriage M2. This was followed by the M2A1 which had the gear ratios in the elevating and traversing mechanisms changed so that the gun could move faster. The gun itself was unchanged, apart from changing some dimensions and screw threads to US standards.

The arrival of the proximity fuze not only improved the accuracy of gunfire but also improved the rate of fire by removing one function – fuze setting – from the operating cycle of the gun; it also removed a variable – the dead time – from the calculation of future position. And in the summer of 1944 it occurred to the US Army that it ought to be possible to develop a new gun that took advantage of all this. In August 1944 an urgent requirement was stated for 'a short and intermediate range AA gun compatible with the VT fuze'. The calibre was specified as 75mm, since this was considered to

The Twilight of the Gods. US 90mm M2 guns of the 63rd AAA Battalion at practice at the US Army range on the Baltic in July 1956.

Other than some minor differences in the carriage and sights there was little to distinguish between the US Bofors M1 and the Bofors guns of other countries. This one was protecting the airstrip on Guadalcanal in 1944.

be the smallest shell that would accept a VT fuze and still have sufficient explosive inside it to give the shell a useful lethal area; VT fuzes at that stage of their development had a far deeper intrusion into the shell than did conventional fuzes and thus displaced about 6 to 8oz (170–225g) of filling. Pilot models were to be built in both towed and self-propelled types, with and without fire control on the mounting, so covering all the various possibilities.

The 75mm T22 gun was designed quite rapidly and by January 1945 a number of guns were waiting mountings at Watervliet Arsenal. The only cloud on the horizon was that they developed a muzzle velocity of only 2,300ft/sec (700m/sec), which was not much of a perfor-

mance for an anti-aircraft gun, and by June 1945 there was talk of re-designing the gun to achieve 3,000ft/sec (915m/sec) velocity. In August 1945 the T22E1 gun was proposed, ten calibres longer (fifty instead of forty) in an attempt to get more velocity.

The Carriage T18 was proposed in September 1944 as the short-term solution, a towed mounting with off-carriage fire control but with remote power control of the gun. The T19 carriage was the long-term solution, another towed mounting but with on-mounting fire-control equipment. This began as an optical tracker and predictor, but gradually grew until a complete radar tracker, optical sight and predictor unit was fitted on to the carriage.

The 75mm M51 Skysweeper as it finally appeared in the textbooks.

155

The M51 as it appeared in the flesh; a gun at the Kaiserslautern range in Germany in 1956. The target is being optically tracked and the range measured by radar as the gun prepares to fire.

The gun was to be fed from two rotating magazines, which delivered rounds to a central loading tray from where they were rammed into the breech, and a rate of forty-five rounds per minute was achieved. But the velocity stayed at 2,300ft/sec, and this was simply not good enough. By the time all these components had been married together and the guns tested, the war was over and the whole project was halted. The gun and ammunition designers were told to get the muzzle velocity up to 3,000ft/sec while the carriage went back for a complete re-think, because in 1945 the science of radar was advancing so fast that by the time a new radar set had been built it was virtually obsolete. It was to be several years before the T22 project got into the hands of the soldiers.

The M51 in retirement; perhaps the sole remaining specimen. At Aberdeen Proving Ground in the USA.

5   The Electro-Optical Revolution

The guided missile is not the subject of this book and I do not intend to get involved with it, but we have to acknowledge its existence, since the shadow of the missile in the decade after World War Two ended the development of heavy AA artillery and very nearly caused the demise of light guns as well.

Germany spent the last year of the war reviewing its anti-aircraft weapon technology and came to some surprising conclusions; one, for example, was that you stood a better chance of downing a bomber by using impact fuzes instead of time fuzes. This theory was advanced by a German Air Ministry scientist, backed by impeccable statistics, showing that the chances of bursting a shell close enough to an aircraft to damage it were more or less the same as the chances of a direct hit. So if you removed the fuze-setting errors from the predication equation, and removed the need for 'dead time', you would firstly make the shooting more accurate and you would also step up the rate of fire. The conclusion was that an impact-fuzed shell actually stood a better chance of bringing down an aircraft than did a time-fuzed shell.

Bearing in mind that time fuzes had been one of the fundamentals of anti-aircraft fire since 1914, one can understand that such a revolutionary theory met with a degree of disbelief. But the statistics were carefully examined by other scientists and pronounced correct, and a series of firing trials took place, which showed that, in fact, the scientist had rather understated his case. In March 1945, orders were given for all flak batteries to discontinue the use of time fuzes and adopt percussion fuzes with self-destruction instead. But by that time it was too late for any meaningful results to be obtained from which to assess the worth of the idea. It was subsequently examined in Britain and pronounced valid, but by that time the proximity fuze had taken the field and the theory was not pursued.

The Germans also reached the conclusion that a guided pilotless machine carrying a sizeable warhead and fitted with a proximity fuze was, for all its expense, a more cost-effective way of destroying a four-engined bomber and its cargo than either anti-aircraft guns or fighter aircraft. And since the Allied air bombardment was reaching serious proportions by the summer of 1944, massive effort was thrown into the development of air-defence missiles. The Germans were thus the first people to discover the enormous time-lag between what the missile designer puts on paper and what the soldier gets to fire at the enemy. Although one or two missiles were, reputedly, fired at Allied aircraft in the final weeks of the war, they do not appear to have been noticed by their targets and scarcely any of the missile programmes were beyond what we would now call the advanced development stage. Generally, they had been flown, but such matters as control and fuzing were still the subject of debate and experiment.

Nevertheless, the results, considering the short time and limited resources available, were impressive, and the aircraft industry around the world took notice when the war ended and the research became public. This was obviously the way to go and the 'steam age' of gunnery would be jettisoned just as soon as the few niggling bugs had been ironed out of the projects. Unfortunately the bugs took rather more ironing than had been expected, and the heavy gun remained a viable proposition for another ten years.

157

Analysis of wartime experience with medium and heavy guns appeared to show that most of the ballistic problems were either solved or within sight of being solved; the greatest remaining problem was that of shell density – getting sufficient metal into the air around the target to ensure some of it hitting the target. The solution was approachable from three directions: heavier guns firing heavier shells; more of the existing guns; or faster-firing guns. But as the German 15cm and 24cm programmes showed, heavier guns were not an easy proposition; like anti-tank guns, they could very easily become too heavy to be practical. More existing guns were thought to be the coward's way out, and an expensive way at that. Which left the prospect of making the existing guns fire faster. Which led, in Britain, to 'Project Ratefixer'.

Ratefixer was a long-term trial that was aimed at getting the highest possible rate of fire out of a standard 3.7-inch Mark 6 gun. Earlier attempts at mechanical loading – as, for example, the 6-pounder intermediate gun – had simply sought to reproduce the same sequence of events as hand loading – open the breech, eject the spent case, present the fresh round, ram it, close the breech, fire the gun – but use machinery to make it faster. It had then been suggested that this might not necessarily be the right solution. For example, it might be possible to begin presenting the fresh round while the gun was being fired, and so arrange the paths of the incoming round and the ejecting case that they passed each other in mid-flight. Four different designs were built: 'Ratefixer K', designed by Captain Kulikowski of the Polish Resettlement Corps, used two drums at 90 degrees to the mounting, feeding alternating arms which swung the cartridges across to a central rammer; 'Ratefixer C', by Colonel Carmichael, REME, used a thirty-round hopper feeding a cross-table and then through a 1.5m (5ft) diameter trunnion; 'Ratefixer CR', by Mr Russell Robinson, a noted machine-gun designer, was the 'C' model modified to belt

feed; and 'Ratefixer CN', by Frazer-Nash, was belt-fed and powered by an hydraulic motor.

These experimental weapons all worked well (although film exists of 'K' blotting its copybook by going berserk and throwing live rounds all over the trials ground), and 'CN' eventually reached a rate of fire of seventy-five rounds per minute, which was no mean feat, considering the complete 3.7-inch Mark 6 cartridge weighed some 62.5lb (28.4kg) and meant shifting some 2.5 tons of ammunition a minute. But by 1949, when the project was completed it was obvious that, while the exercise had been of great value in solving the loading problem, the gun was now becoming obsolescent and an improved weapon would have to be developed before the project could be taken any further.

The principal demand was for high velocity, leading to a short time of flight and hence an easier ballistic problem and a better chance of hitting. A good deal had been learned about the production of high velocity during the wartime development of anti-tank guns, and two solutions presented themselves – a taper bore or a sabot projectile.

The taper-bore gun is just what the name suggests, a gun with a barrel, the calibre of which reduces as it approaches the muzzle. It could, for example, have a 3-inch calibre at the breech and a 2-inch calibre at the muzzle. As you might expect, boring and rifling a tapering hole is not something to be attempted lightly, and the ammunition has to be designed to conform with the reducing calibre, but it can be done and the Germans put a number of taper-bore guns into service. The benefit arises from the fact that the gas pressure in the bore of the gun remains the same but, because the diameter of the shot decreases, the unit pressure – pounds per square inch – increases and thus increases the velocity.

The sabot solution simply means firing a sub-calibre projectile inside a full-calibre lightweight casing that is discarded at the gun muzzle, so that in the bore the weight/diameter ratio is favourable to fast acceleration, while outside the bore the ratio changes to one favourable to sustaining momentum over a long distance.

And so, in order to cover all possible options, two solutions were chosen. Firstly a taper-bore gun, with the calibre reducing from 4.26in to 3.2in (11cm to 8cm) would be developed by Vickers, and secondly a 5-inch gun using a fin-stabilized 'dart' shell' would be developed by the Royal Armaments Research and Development Establishment. But progress on the 4.26/3.2 model was slow – it was, after all, a difficult problem to solve – and a conventional gun was put in hand, to fit the same mounting as the taper-bore weapon, as a form of insurance. This became the 'Gun 102mm X1' but it too was dogged by delays in development; it was not ready until 1956, was a failure, and it was abandoned in 1957. The 4.26/3.2 idea was also scrapped as being unworkable.

The 5-inch gun, now known as 'Green Mace', was an enormous piece of machinery with two rotary magazines behind it feeding to a common loading tray, a system with some resemblance to the American 'Skysweeper', but firing a much heavier round. The projectile was a long and slender fin-stabilized shell with a proximity fuze, supported in the bore by its oversize fins and a central 144-piece sabot. The gun was water-cooled, was completely power-operated remotely from the predictor, and had only one man on it when firing, seated in a glassed-in cabin rather like a tractor driver and doing little more than monitoring the system as it operated. Its highest rate of fire was about

'Green Mace', the 5-inch fast-firing heavy gun, never got beyond the prototype stage. It currently resides at the Imperial War Museum at Duxford in Cambridgeshire for those who wish to see the 'Last of the Dinosaurs'.

seventy-five rounds per minute, which was quite astonishing for a weapon of such a size, and there seems little doubt that it would have done all that was asked of it. But it completed its trials in 1956 and the design was then abandoned; not the least of the problems was that it weighed 28 tons and was of a size that would go under few railway bridges.

Meanwhile another weapon had appeared, the 'Gun X4' or 'Longhand', which was a 3.7-inch Mark 6 resurrected and fitted with a twelve-round rapid-loading conveyor. This got as far as being approved for service introduction on 15 February 1957, but nothing further was done, and in 1958 a policy statement was promulgated: there would be 'no further attempts at a cannon solution for medium or heavy anti-aircraft defence'. The guided missile was now ready and waiting in the wings.

America reviewed the situation in the late 1940s and came to the conclusion that their existing 75mm 'Skysweeper', 90mm M2 and 120mm M1 guns would see them through the interim period before they could get their missiles into service, and in this they were gambling on their speed of development being as good as the engineers and scientists were promising. In the event, they were not far wrong and no new designs of gun ever appeared in the USA. The 'Skysweeper' was eventually perfected and entered service in the middle 1950s, but its velocity never reached the magical 3,000ft/sec (915m/sec) figure that had been hoped. The service version, known as the 75mm Gun M51, fired a 15lb (6.8kg) HE shell at 2,800ft/sec (850m/sec) to reach 30,000ft (9,000m) effective ceiling, with a rate of fire of forty-five rounds per minute. It went out of service with the US Army in the mid-1970s, and lingered slightly longer in Japan and Turkey.

France and Germany, of course, and most of the remainder of Europe, had nothing to worry about: they had no anti-aircraft guns after 1945. In the immediate post-war period they relied upon the Allied occupation forces to provide air

defence and when they revived their own defensive forces they were initially armed with American guns. Again, this filled the gap until they could get their missile defences into working order. The Americans also shipped a number of 120mm gun batteries across to Germany for some years in the 1950s and early 1960s, the only time these weapons were ever deployed outside the Continental USA.

Which leaves Russia's post-war activity to be accounted for; there was not a great deal of it, but it had some interesting aspects. The 76mm and 85mm guns had been satisfactory during the war because Germany had no strategic bombing forces and no aircraft capable of deep penetration into Soviet Russia; therefore the only requirement was a mobile gun for the field armies and the protection of forward cities. But in the post-war world, with heavier and longer-ranging aircraft appearing, particularly in the hands of people whom the Soviets didn't particularly like or trust, a new and more powerful air-defence gun was an obvious requirement. This resulted in the 100mm KS-19 gun appearing in about 1950; it was first used to arm home defence batteries in the USSR, after which numbers were exported to other Communist countries, and it was built under licence in China. A quite conventional design, it nevertheless incorporated all the best ideas that the war had brought forth, and it bore some slight resemblance to the 88mm Flak 41 in being rear-trunnioned and on a turntable rather than the more usual pedestal mounting. Remote power operation, with power ramming and mechanical fuze-setting, the latter resembling that of the British 3.7-inch guns, completed the package, which was on the usual sort of four-wheeled platform with outriggers. Maximum ceiling was claimed as 50,000ft (15,250m), effective ceiling 45,000ft (13,700m) with a proximity fuze, and the gun fired a 15.6kg (34lb) shell at 900m/sec (3,000ft/sec).

Whilst the 100mm gun was seen as the future field-army weapon, it was appreciated that something heavier was needed for prime vulnerable